OJIBWA

Michael G. Johnson

OJIBWA

People of Forests and Prairies

FIREFLY BOOKS

A FIREFLY BOOK

Published by Firefly Books Ltd. 2016

First printing

Publisher Cataloging-in-Publication Data (U.S.)

Names: Johnson, Michael G., author.
Title: Ojibwa : people of forests and prairies / Michael G. Johnson.
Description: Richmond Hill, Ontario, Canada : Firefly Books, 2016.
| Includes bibliography and index. | Summary: "Comprehensive and authoritative description and exploration of all aspects, historic and contemporary, of Ojibwa culture and history" — Provided by publisher.
Identifiers: ISBN 978-1-77085-800-8 (hardcover)
Subjects: LCSH: Ojibwa Indians.
Classification: LCC E99.C6J646 |DDC 970.00497 – dc23

Library and Archives Canada Cataloguing in Publication

Johnson, Michael, 1937 April 22–, author
    Ojibwa : people of forests and prairies / Michael G. Johnson.
Includes bibliographical references and index.
ISBN 978-1-77085-800-8 (bound)
    1. Ojibwa Indians — History. 2. Ojibwa Indians — Social life and customs. I. Title.
E99.C6J59 2016   970.004'97333   C2016-900572-0

Published in the United States by
Firefly Books (U.S.) Inc.
P.O. Box 1338, Ellicott Station
Buffalo, New York 14205

Published in Canada by
Firefly Books Ltd.
50 Staples Avenue, Unit 1
Richmond Hill, Ontario L4B 0A7

Printed in China

This book is dedicated to the memory of Ian West, a friend and colleague.

Credits & Acknowledgments
All photographs and artifacts are from the M.G. Johnson Collection unless credited otherwise (in italics at the end of the caption). Photography was by Simon Clay. The artwork on pp. 98–100 was prepared by Jonathan Smith. Maps and drawings unless credited otherwise are by Mark Franklin from M.G. Johnson originals. Design is by Eleanor Forty.

Friends and colleagues who have helped with this project are: in the United States Dr. James H. Howard, Samuel Cahoon, Louis Garcia, Neil Oppendike, Dr. James A. Clifton, Siobhan Marks, and Dr. Marcia Anderson.

In Canada: Arni Brownstone, Dr. Cath Oberholtzer, David Sager, Frank Kodras, and John Hellson.

In the UK: Dennis Burdett, Mark Sykes, Leo and Vanessa Woods, Dr. Colin Taylor, Richard Green, and John Datlen.

Also to my family for their enduring patience, Nancy, Polly, Adam, and Grace; and to the memory of Sarah.

Cover photo: © Smithsonian American Art Museum, Washington DC / Art Resource, NY

Page 2: Henry Inman copy of a Charles Bird King painting of St. Croix Ojibwa chief, c. 1826, for McKenney and Hall, Vol. III. He sports a fringed hairstyle popular with Ojibwa men of the early 19th century and wears non native ostrich (most likely) and peacock feathers in his hair. These would have been obtained from traders. Charles Bird King (1785–1862) was the official painter of Indian delegates to Washington D.C. from many tribes in formal negotiations with the War Department during the 1820s and 1830s. He and George Cooke also copied the slightly earlier works of James Otto Lewis painted in the Midwest. These paintings were transferred from the War Department to the Smithsonian Institution where they were destroyed by fire in 1865. However, despite the loss, many of King's paintings had been copied by King himself and Henry Inman for the three-volume epic by T.L. McKenney and J. Hall *History of the Indian Tribes of North America* (1836–1844).

Contents

Introduction

GREAT LAKES PEOPLE BEFORE EUROPEANS ARRIVED

Prehistoric Great Lakes Indians have left archaeological remains from a time known as the Boreal Archaic period that lasted from 5000 BCE to about 500 BCE. During this period some Great Lakes peoples were making use of copper for the manufacture of some weapons and tools. These so-called Old Copper Indians mined and made copper implements on both sides of Lake Superior. Copper was extracted from its matrix rock by fire, broken down with beach boulders, and fashioned into tools and weapons by cold-hammering, producing spear points, knives, fishing hooks, and barbed harpoon points. They hunted deer, elk, and caribou and seem to have been among the first on the continent to use dogs. Other forest-adapted cultures possessed new kinds of woodworking tools that had been lacking among the Paleo-Indians who had preceded them. Stone ax, adze, and gouge were produced by flaking or chipping into shape. They hunted with spears hurled with the aid of a spear-thrower.

Between 1500 BCE and 500 BCE significant new influences affected the southern perimeter of the Great Lakes region. Arriving from the south, these influences included pottery and the use of burial mounds built over the graves of the dead. The Indians of this Early Woodland Period continued to obtain food by hunting, fishing, and gathering, but also produced refined copper beads, polished stone, slate, and shell ornaments for personal adornment.

The Hopewellian Culture had its principal centers in the valleys of the Ohio and Illinois rivers c. 300 BCE–CE 700 where it built the most impressive burial mounds holding the remains of important personages. From far and wide the Hopewellians obtained precious substances: conch shells, pearls from rivers, obsidian from the Rockies, mica and copper via trade through a vast network of trails. The Early Woodland Indians were not exempt from such outside influences. Hopewell culture was based on agricultural produce, which had arrived in parts of North America north of the Rio Grande from Meso-America: beans, squash, and finally maize (Indian corn). Corn became the sustainer of many Indian peoples and also a cultural theme of their ceremonial life. Although corn-farming gradually diffused

Above: *Deputation of Indians from the Chippewa Tribes to the President of Upper Canada, Maj-Gen. Sir Frederic Ph. Robinson, K.C.B., 1815.* Group of warriors, one using a military drum and one dancing. Painting by Rudolph Steiger 1791–1824, National Gallery of Canada.

Right: *Ojibwa Indian Camp, Northern Shore of Lake Huron,* by Frederick Arthur Verner (1836–1928). The painting shows a peaked birchbark wigwam, canoe, basket, and woman holding a cradleboard.

to various parts of the Woodlands, its northern spread was limited by climatic conditions. Hopewellians produced refined tools and weapons made of stone, copper, and bone, as well as ceremonial tobacco pipes made of polished stone and carved in the form of animals and humans, and ceremonial pottery.

The Late Woodland Period CE 800 to CE 1600 in the upper Great Lakes was characterized by a number of localized phases which developed in situ, and some that entered the region. These have been identified by effigy mounds, burial mounds, and ornaments. Such cultures are Aztalan (now Southern Wisconsin), and from around Georgian Bay, Ontario. Within this late Woodland tradition two main sub-traditions emerged: one Iroquoian and the other (less documented) Algonkian — the basic Indian cultures of the Woodlands. The Algonkians were ancestors of the Anishinabe.

THE OJIBWA (ANISHINABE)

The language of the Ojibwa people and the closely related Ottawa (Odawa) and Potawatomi languages belong to the vast Algonkian (Algonquian) linguistic family that predominates in the northeastern parts of North America. Oral tradition of a number of Algonkian-speaking peoples place their ancestors living by a great ocean in the process of moving west in the early historic period. A proto-Algonkian language from which all may descend has been suggested to have been spoken about 2,500 to 3,000 years ago.

A number of sub groups within the family have been proposed. The Northeastern and Delaware groups in the list opposite are probably one generic unit within Algonkian, although some doubts exist about its southern limits. The Plains group is, in reality, a geographical group with three very divergent languages. The remaining central area is a mixture of a likely genetic core with others added in the geographical sense. If we exclude the Cree group and the Menominee, the remaining languages probably form another language unit within the family. Within this unit are the Ojibwa group with the very closely related Ojibwa, Ottawa, and Potawatomi languages which have been reported by some authorities as likely one language and people some point in pre history. Oral traditions tend to support this theory.

The Algonkian family has also been linked to the Yurok and Wiyot languages of northern California and to the Beothuk tongue once spoken in Newfoundland into a larger phylum called Algic.

THE ALGONKIAN LANGUAGES

Plains Group
North Blackfoot, Piegan, Blood; Arapaho, Atsina (Gros Ventre); Cheyenne, Sutaio.

Cree Group
Montagnais, Nascapi, East Cree (East Main Cree), Attikamek; West Cree (West Main Cree, inc. Moosonee), Swampy Cree, Woods Cree; Plains Cree.

Central Group
Menominee; Sauk, Fox; Kickapoo, Mascouten; Illini, Miami, Wea; Shawnee.

Ojibwa (Anishinabe) Group
Algonkin (Algonquin), Ojibwa (Mississauga, Northern Ojibwa, Chippewa, Saulteaux, Bungi), Ottawa, Nipissing, Potawatomi.

Northeastern Group
Micmac (Mi'kmaq); Malecite, Passamaquoddy; Eastern Abenaki, Penobscot; Western Abenaki, Sokoki, Pennacook, Etchemin (possibly 2 dialects); Massachusett, Nipmuc, Pocomtuc; Wampanoag, Nauset; Narragansett, Niantic; Mohegan, Pequot; Quiripi (Tunxis, Paugussett); Unquachog (Montauk, Shinnecock).

Delaware Group
Mahican, Wappinger; Delaware (2 dialects); Nanticoke, Conoy.
Powhatan (possibly several dialects).
Carolina (possibly several dialects).

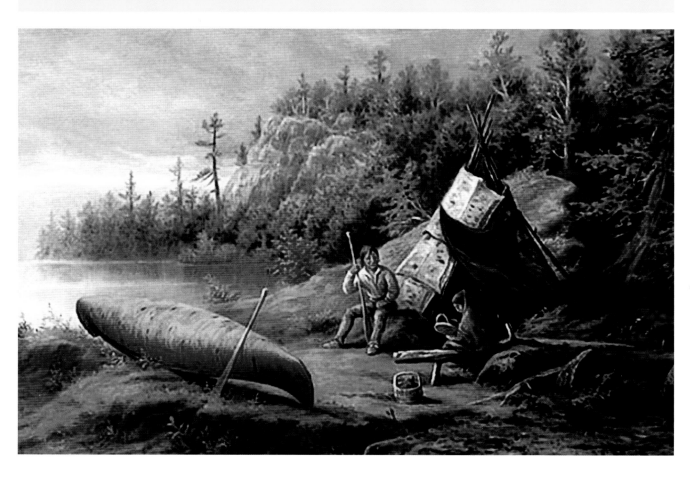

Above: "Ojibwa family," photographed by famed Kenora, Ontario photographer Carl G. Linde, who documented many facets of native life in the early 20th century.

Despite a number of proposals for the historical reconstructions for these languages, it is clear the greater levels of divergence are found further west since they constitute the earliest branches in the westward migration of Algonkian peoples. The smaller divergence occurs generally among the eastern tribes. In recent times there has also been extensive mixing of Cree and Ojibwa, particularly in Canada.

OJIBWA LAND

At the zenith of their geographical expansion about 1800, the Ojibwa people claimed an estate probably greater than any other native American people of North America north of the Rio Grande, with the possible exception of the Cree, their Algonkian-speaking relatives and northern neighbors. Their habitat in the Canadian Shield was a land of coniferous forest of spruce, poplar, hemlock, birch, tamarac, pine, and ash. This land is upwards of 1,000 feet high, flat-lying with hills, huge numbers of lakes and rivers, some shallow and marshy, some with rocky shorelines, having often cold and extremely clear water. The coniferous forest zone extended south to central present-day Minnesota and parts of northern Wisconsin and Michigan where it gave way to a mixture of coniferous and deciduous forest, adding maple, elm, beech, oak, and hickory, and hence to a southern perimeter of deciduous forest and, finally, Grasslands and Prairie.

In Canada the Ojibwa western bands penetrated the Parklands region, a transitional zone of mixed prairie, woodland, hills, and pastures that formed an immense boundary between the forests of the north and the Grasslands of the south. The Grasslands region, in relation to North America, encompasses both the tall grass Prairies and short grass High Plains that were home to the Assiniboine, Blackfoot, and branches of the Sioux.

By the close of the 18th century the Ojibwa had adapted to these varying geographical regions — Woodland, Parkland, and Grassland — but were to remain a predominantly Woodland people; their northern bands occupying the upper branches of a river system draining into the James and Hudson bays, and their southern bands in a drainage area dominated by rivers running into the upper Mississippi Valley and Great Lakes. This land of countless rivers and lakes facilitated relatively swift travel over huge distances by bark canoes.

Below: Plains Ojibwa woman Kei-a-gis-gis, wife of "The Six" (see p. 156) after George Catlin, painted at Fort Union, 1832.

Temperatures vary from a mean summer temperature of 60°F (15°C) (in a range of 40 to 80°F [4–26°C]) to a winter mean of −10°F (23°C) (in a range of −40 to 20°F [40–6°C]). Freeze-up occurs November through April, when the snow and ice begin to melt. As a result there was limited use of corn (maize) that could only be grown in locations with at least 140 frost-free days. This restricted its range to the perimeters of Lake Huron and Georgian Bay. Huge areas of edible wild rice were harvested extending from Rice Lake, Ontario, through northern Wisconsin and Minnesota beyond Lake of the Woods.

Two large game species were found in the northern coniferous forests: caribou and moose. Smaller game included otter, mink, muskrat, beaver, and lynx. By contrast, southern areas included mule deer, wapiti (elk), and in the Parkland and Prairie, pronghorn antelope and bison (buffalo). Fish was an important resource in all areas and were plentiful in lakes and rivers. Beaver could be trapped in shallow ponds and was often eaten. Birds, particularly goose and turkey, were also caught and eaten. Nuts were added to their subsistence supplements and in the north berries were collected. Wild plant foods were gathered and maple sugar sap collected.

Ojibwa in the conifer regions used birchbark to cover their canoes and their various forms of wigwams, and in the south made dugout canoes and frequently used elm bark or reeds to cover their domestic dwellings.

The Southwestern Ojibwa, primarily called "Chippewa" by the Americans, are often regarded as the nucleus of traditional native Woodland Indian culture.

Below: The land of the Ojibwa in the 17th to 19th centuries.

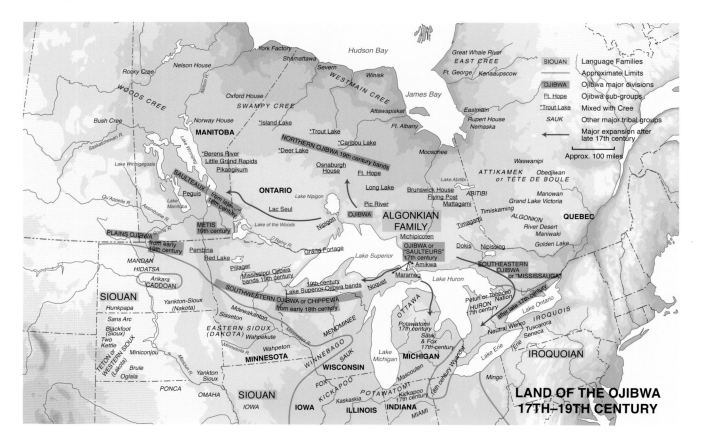

LAND OF THE OJIBWA 17TH–19TH CENTURY

Chapter 1: History

Above: Woodland Ojibwa man, Nijogijig, c. 1880. He holds a carved and "twisted" wooden pipe stem. The twisted section is actually carved.

Today approximately one third of a million people are descendants of the numerous bands of the Ojibwa Indian people. Many are enrolled members of reservation agencies within the U.S. or registered as band members of First Nation reserves in Canada. Others are self-identified in the U.S. census, or in Métis communities in both the U.S. and Canada. However, the discriminative government policies in both countries has resulted in differing requirements for Indian status. Nevertheless, the Ojibwa challenge the Navajo and Cherokee as the largest "tribe" today north of Mexico and likely the largest taken as a whole before European contact.

Another problem has been the many names that have been used to describe the Ojibwa over the years, and in many different places. Ojibwa is the term most used in ethnographical literature (and is used in this book), but now often replaced with Ojibwe in recent studies. In the U.S. the government in their dealings at treaties and later reservation administration have used the term "Chippewa," whereas the Canadians used Ojibway for many years. In the Lake Winnipeg area and beyond, they are often known as Saulteaux (pronounced Sotoe), others use Plains Ojibwa or Bungi. On the eastern shore of Georgian Bay they are known as Mississauga and elsewhere in Ontario "Cree-Chip" where the two peoples have intermarried over the years.

The most consistent explanation of the terms Ojibwa or Chippewa connects with "puckered up," a reference to the seams in moccasin construction, although this has been challenged by various writers.

Many Ojibwa identify themselves as *Anishinaubag* (*Anishinabe*) meaning "original men" in their own tongue. The French had contributed more than 30 names to various bands by the middle of the 17th century having contacted them shortly after the founding of Quebec. French Jesuits had arrived at Sault Ste. Marie in 1640 and called the local Ojibwa *saulteurs* (people of the rapids). They had also opened a mission on Manitoulin Island by 1648. The perimeter of Lake Huron seems to have been their homeland during this period and a central area for a number of Algonkian-speaking peoples including the Ottawa (Odawa) and Potawatomi, who claim to have a special relationship with the Ojibwa, sharing a related language, and at times an alliance called the Three Fires. There were, and still are, several dialects of the Ojibwa language.

Left: *Scene in an Indian Tent*, a painting by Peter Rindisbacher, probably showing Plains Ojibwa and Métis, men, women, and children, inside a tipi, 1820s. The man on the right wears a fitted skin coat with porcupine quillwork at the shoulder. By this time such coats had incorporated additional European features such as collars and cuffs. Rindisbacher (1806–1834) lived in Manitoba and what is now Wisconsin.

Below Left: *Tent at Red River*, by Peter Rindisbacher, c. 1825. It was done during his residence at Red River colony (Manitoba) where he was an eyewitness to the Cree, Ojibwa, Assiniboine, and Sioux, as well as the Métis and white traders who traded and lived there. In the process Rindisbacher was one of the first artists to depict the inside of a Plains Indian tipi.
 The Indians depicted, probably Plains Ojibwa, have objects and dress that clearly show their transitional culture between Woodland and Plains. Birchbark vessels, a child's cradle, and trade cloth men's leggings indicate their Woodland culture background; whereas a painted buffalo robe, skin leggings, and a chest disk on a skin shirt refers to their Plains orientation. Note on the floor two Passenger Pigeons — hunted to extinction in the 19th century, the last captive bird dying in 1914.

The expansion of the Ojibwa into their later geographical range — to the southern shores of Lake Superior, into the southern Ontario peninsula, and west to the Lake of the Woods area — was due principally to the expanding fur trade and as a result of the various conflicts between the French and the British. The Indian tribes who exchanged furs — particularly beaver pelts — for coveted European goods greatly increased their power. Iron and copper receptacles were more durable than those of clay or stone; wool, cloth, and thread became available to replace buckskin and sinew, but most important of all, firearms revolutionized hunting and warfare.

Above: Emanuel Leutze's 1858 painting *Washington at the Battle of the Monongahela* shows the defeat of the British Army on July 9, 1755, at the hands of Native Americans and French-Canadians. The British commander, Gen. Edward Braddock III, died a few days later on July 13.

Opposite: Map of Plains Ojibwa/ Saulteaux expansion west into the lands also occupied by Plains Cree and Assiniboine.

By the 1640s the French had established a burgeoning fur trade with the Huron in the Nottawasaga Bay area, and the Dutch with the Iroquois in what is now New York State. Since much of the Iroquois homeland had already been trapped out by this time, the Iroquois invaded Huron territory dispersing or destroying them and other local related tribes (1649–1656). The relationship the Ojibwa had with the former Huron middlemen now brought them into conflict with the Iroquois. The Iroquois continued their attacks north and west, but the Ojibwa's seminomadic way of life — in contrast to the Huron's sedentary lifestyle — allowed them to fight a relatively successful defensive war and retreat to the area of Lake Superior. By the late 17th century they were back on Manitoulin Island and later drove the Iroquois from southern Ontario. In the south they had established themselves on the upper and lower peninsulas of Michigan, and in the west had established settlements in Keweenaw Bay and the strategically positioned Chequamegon Bay, a key to future southwestern expansion. Ojibwa bands north of Lake Superior — usually small bands heavily dependent on hunting — also began moving west, ultimately to the western end of Lake Superior and to the Lake of the Woods region. The French explorers and fur traders with Indian guides had successfully managed the use of the old Indian trails and canoe routes from Quebec and Montreal through a network of rivers and lakes to the Mississippi River with only a few portages. The Jesuit fathers, who had established missions in the region, recorded the first descriptions of Indian life in the Great Lakes area and they augmented French control driven by the acquisition of furs.

In 1701, at Montreal, the Iroquois and other tribes agreed to a general peace with the French and likewise agreed with the British at

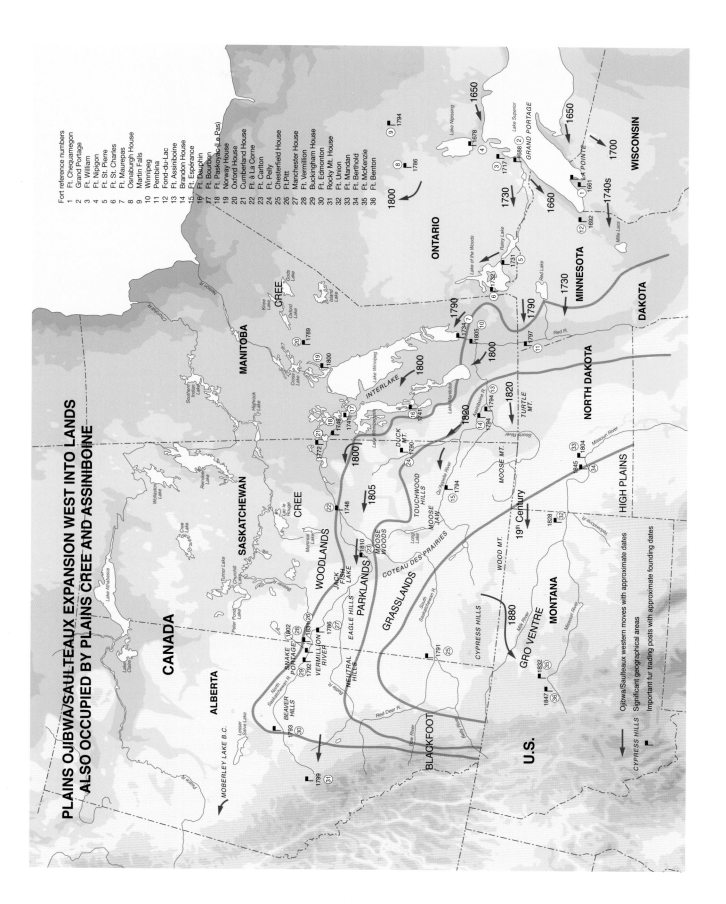

Albany shortly afterwards. From that time until the fall of New France in 1760, the Ojibwa experienced perhaps a golden age of trade, presents, and plunder without any settlement pressure from Europeans. They had good relationships with the French fur traders, who often married native women, but cheaper English trade goods kept British influence in the Ohio country as the Indians vacillated in order to obtain better goods and presents.

Ojibwa warriors fought against the British in 1745–1746 and were among Langlade's warriors who destroyed Pickawillany (a Pennsylvania-controlled trading post in the Ohio Country) in 1752, and were again with the French when Gen. Edward Braddock was defeated at the Monongahela River in July 1755. They were also among Montcalm's Indian allies at Fort William Henry in 1757 during the French and Indian War (1754–1760). They were very active in Pontiac's coalition of Indian tribes who rebelled against the negative aspects of British influence that saw Indians capture eight forts in the Ohio Country in 1763. During the American Revolution many Indian groups remained neutral, but pressured by both British and Americans to join their respective sides a number of Ojibwa joined the British. In the War of 1812 Ojibwa, Ottawa, and Iroquois fought for the British, the last time they participated in a colonial conflict.

In the northwest, Ojibwa villages had been established at Thunder Bay and Rainy Lake by the 1730s advancing towards Lake of the Woods and ultimately the Canadian Parklands. From the southern shore of Lake Superior the Ojibwa spread south bringing them into conflict with the Dakota (Santee Sioux) for the wild rice growing areas in the drainages of the Wisconsin, Chippewa, St. Croix, and upper Mississippi rivers. They had established villages at Lac du Flambeau, Lac Courte Oreilles, Fond du Lac, and Mille Lacs by the mid-18th century. By the end of the century the Sioux had been removed from Wisconsin and much of northern Minnesota but the conflict continued until the mid-19th century.

Among the explanations given for Ojibwa motives for moving west from the Lake of the Woods and other locations to the Canadian Parklands and marginal Plains were to access richer beaver areas, further food sources, and the effects of the smallpox outbreaks of 1780–1783, during which, according to reports from traders, half the Ojibwa west and north of Grand Portage died. Perhaps during this period the origins of the curative Midewiwin Society can be found (however, many believe it was an aboriginal organization), which reinforced social and religious ties spreading a common body of heritage. Their traditional life cycle of

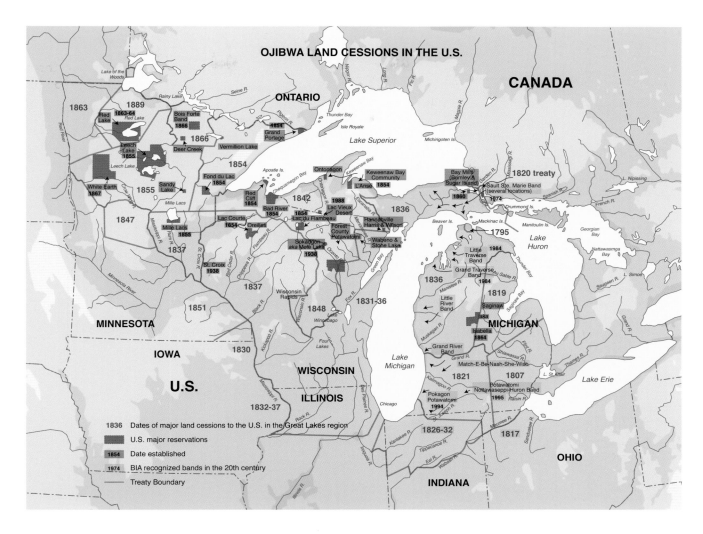

hunting, fishing, gathering wild rice, and visiting trading posts for winter supplies continued in their new locations. By the 1790s these included the eastern shore of Lake Winnipeg, the interlake area between Lakes Winnipeg, Winnipegosis, and Manitoba then spreading out across an enormous territory including the Red River, Assiniboine, and Qu'Appelle rivers, Turtle Mountain, and along the north Saskatchewan to Edmonton House and the Rockies. To a degree the Ojibwa favored the North West Company as a trading organization rather than their rivals, the Hudson's Bay Company — historically connected to the Cree — until their merger in 1821. These western Ojibwa were now mixing and trading with the Plains-orientated Cree and Assiniboine who, in turn, were exchanging goods for horses with the Mandan Indians on the upper Missouri River.

Some western bands now became increasingly reliant on the bison for meat during lean seasons but many groups continued to harvest wild rice, fish, and gather vegetal products. A number, however, switched gradually to typical Plains culture influenced by the Plains Cree and Assiniboine with whom they subsequently intermarried. They adopted the Sun Dance ritual, clown cults, warrior societies, horses, horse gear, tipis, bison robes, and Red

continued on p. 20

Above: Land cessions in the U.S.

Opposite, Above: Col. Henry Bouquet, a Swiss-born British officer, in council with Indians of Pontiac's confederacy, probably on the Muskingum River in Ohio country in 1764.

Opposite, Below: The British commander of the fort at Detroit in 1763 was Major (later Major-General) Henry Gladwin (1729–1791). The Indians attempted to take the fort by stealth, requesting meetings with Gladwin while concealing their weapons. Legend has it that he was forewarned of Pontiac's plan by an Ojibwa girl, apparently his mistress. Painting by John Hall.

WAR OF 1812: MILITARY ENGAGEMENTS WITH INDIAN INVOLVEMENT

	Location	State	Date	Notes
1	Prophetstown	IND	Nov 1811	Harrison's dispersal of Indians under Tenskwatawa (the Prophet)
2	Gilberts Lick	MO	June 1812	
3	Ft. Mackinac	MICH	July 1812	Surrender of Americans to Indians, Métis & fur traders
4	Canard River	ONT	July 1812	
5	Brownstown Creek	MICH	Aug 1812	Americans held their own against British & Indians under Tecumseh
6	Swan Creek	MICH	Aug 1812	
7	Monguagon	MICH	Aug 1812	
8	Ft. Dearborn, Chicago	ILL	Aug 1812	Massacre of Americans by Indians (mostly Potawatomi)
9	Detroit	MICH	Aug 1812	
10	St. Joseph River	MICH	Sept 1812	
11	Greentown	OHIO	Sept 1812	
12	Ft. St. Mary's	OHIO	Sept 1812	
13	Pigeon Roost	IND	Sept 1812	
14	Ft. Madison	IOWA	Sept 1812	Unsuccessful attempt by Sauks to capture fort
15	Ft. Wayne	IND	Sept 1812	Unsuccessful attempt by 600 warriors to capture fort
16	Mansfield	OHIO	Sept 1812	
17	Ft. Harrison	IND	Sept 1812	American victory under Zacchary Taylor over large force of Indians
18	Blanchard River	OHIO	Sept 1812	
19	Little Turtle's Village	IND	Sept 1812	
20	Elkhart River	IND	Sept 1812	
21	Sandusky River	OHIO	Sept 1812	
22	Peoria	ILL	Oct 1812	
23	Salt River	ILL	Oct 1812	
24	Maumee River	OHIO	Nov 1812	
25	Prophetstown	IND	Nov 1812	Destruction of Indian village
26	Wild Cat Creek	IND	Dec 1812	
27	Big Fire	IND	Dec 1812	
28	Raisin River	MICH	Jan 1813	
29	Ft. Valloria	IND	March 1813	
30	Tipton's Island	IND	March 1813	
31	Mouth of Maumee River	OHIO	May 1813	
32	Ft. Meigs	OHIO	May 1813	
33	Cold Creek	OHIO	June 1813	
34	White River	IND	June 1813	
35	Beaver Dams	ONT	June 1813	
36	*Cape au Gris	ILL	June 1813	
37	Miami Villages Eel River	IND	July 1813	
38	Miami Villages Wabash River	IND	July 1813	
39	Miami Villages Mississinewa River	IND	July 1813	
40	Prophetstown	IND	July 1813	
41	Ft. Madison	IOWA	July 1813	
42	Ft. Meigs	OHIO	July 1813	
43	Lower Sandusky	OHIO	July 1813	
44	Ft. Stephenson	OHIO	Aug 1813	

Above: This marker commemorates the siege during the Pontiac War (1763–1765) during which some British military forts were taken by warriors belonging to a number of tribes in coalition. The siege of Fort Detroit was ultimately unsuccessful.

Location		State	Date	Notes
45	Gomo's	ILL	Sept 1813	
46	Dolsen's Farm	ONT	Oct 1813	
47	Chatham	ONT	Oct 1813	
48	Moraviantown	ONT	Oct 1813	Battle of the Thames, Tecumseh killed
49	Prairie du Chien (Fts. Shelby/Mckay)	WIS	June/July 1814	American occupation then capture by British
50	Saukenuk	ILL	July 1814	Americans v Sauks under Black Hawk
51	Oxford	ONT	Aug 1814	
52	Port Talbot	ONT	Aug 1814	
53	Ft. Mackinac	MICH	Aug 1814	
54	*Boones Lick	MO	Sept 1814	
55	*Miami	MO	Sept 1814	
56	*Cote Sans	MO	Sept 1814	
57	Saukenuk	ILL	Sept 1814	Americans v Sauks under Black Hawk
58	Brant's Ford	ONT	Nov 1814	
59	*Cote Sans	MO	March 1815	
60	*Ft. Howard	MO	May 1815	(Sink Hole) Americans v Sauks under Black Hawk

Key: * = not shown. See map below, War of 1812, battle sites on map Ojibwa Conflicts East and West.

Below: Ojibwa conflicts and main battles.

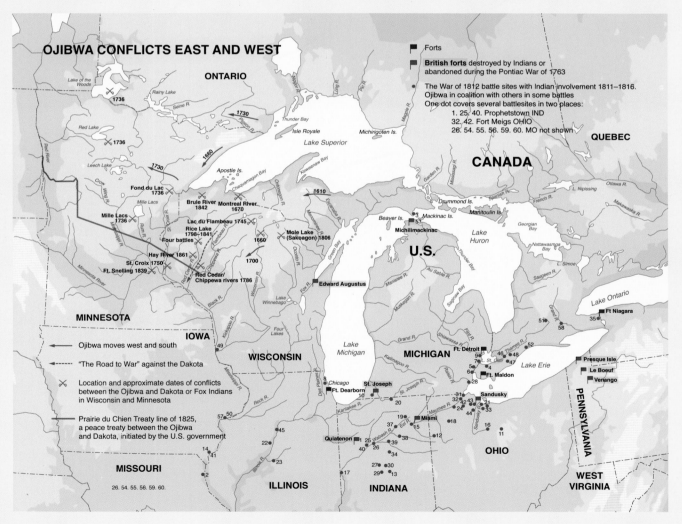

Above: Capt. Andrew H. Bulger, Governor of Assiniboia, and the chiefs and warriors of the "Chippewa tribe of Red Lake" in council in the colony house, Fort Douglas, May 1823, after Peter Rindisbacher.

Opposite: Two groups of Ojibwa visited Europe in the 1840s. Both groups were painted and drawn by George Catlin. They performed their dances for visitors to Catlin's European exhibitions of his paintings. The first group of nine (**Above**) was brought to Great Britain in 1843 by the showman Arthur Rankin and performed for Queen Victoria at Windsor in 1844. These were replaced by a group of Iowas, and in turn succeeded by a second group of 12 Mississauga Ojibwa (**Below**) in 1845 under the leadership of George Henry or Maungwudaus (see p. 24.) Both troupes lost members to smallpox.

River carts from the Métis. Art objects, too, reflected their transitional cultural position. They retained some essentially Woodland artistic traditions, decorating art objects with plant, thunderbird, and animate symbolism, but also adopted the geometric designs of Subarctic Cree and Plains. Both women and men wore some Plains-type buckskin tunics but much clothing was now using European cloth, strouds, wool, and decoration utilizing traded glass beads, silks, and ribbons. Beads were particularly important because of their resonating and reflective qualities. They were sewn and woven to decorate men's and women's attire and superseded porcupine quillwork on religious paraphernalia.

The early decades of the 19th century saw the gradual demise of the fur trade on which many Ojibwa depended. Depleted resources and a shortage of game impelled them to hunt in areas into which white settlers had moved. Diminishing food supplies, hunting restrictions, starvation, and the advancing white settlements forced the Ojibwa to progressively cede their territories to the U.S. government or to the British Crown in Canada:

Area	Ceded
Eastern Ontario	1783–1836
Eastern Michigan and the upper peninsula	1807–1842
Northern and western Wisconsin	1837–1854
Northern Minnesota	1847–1889
South-central Ontario, the Saugeen Peninsula, and Manitoulin Island (except the eastern part of the island)	1850–1862

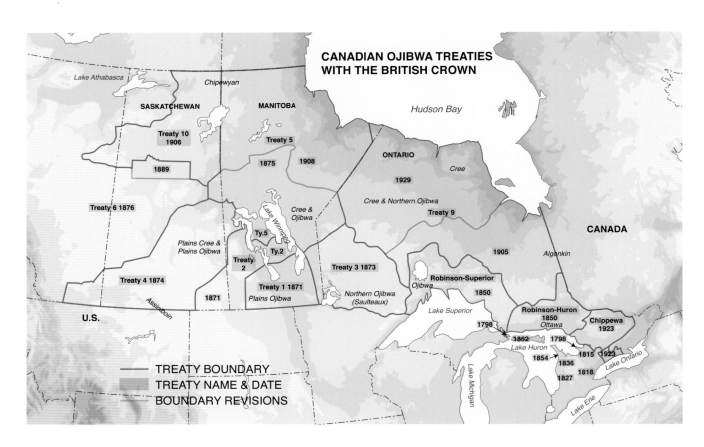

Above: Canadian Ojibwa treaties with the British Crown.

Right: Old Crossing Treaty memorial erected in Huot, MN, in 1932 to commemorate the cession of lands from the "Red Lake and Pembina bands of Chippewa Indians" on October 2, 1863.

The Saulteaux were part of treaties Nos. 1 to 6, which ceded between 1871 and 1890: southern and southwestern Manitoba, Lake of the Woods area, southeastern and central Saskatchewan, and northern Manitoba. They were also part of Treaty No. 9 for Ojibwa of northern Ontario in 1929. Most of the Michigan bands were settled at Isabella, L'Anse, Ontonagon or stayed scattered on the upper peninsula. The Lake Superior bands moved to Lac Courte Oreille, Lac du Flambeau, Bad River, and Red Cliff (later also St. Croix) in Wisconsin; Fond du Lac, Grand Portage, Nett Lake, and Vermilion Lake (Bois Forte bands) in Minnesota. The Mississippi bands moved to Leech Lake, Mille Lacs, White Earth, and Red Lake (including Red Lake, Pembina, and Pillager "Chippewa") reservations in Minnesota. A large group of Pembina and Métis (French-Canadian mixed bloods) were settled at Turtle Mountain, North Dakota. Only one band of Woodland Ojibwa actually left their traditional homelands when a small number accompanied some Munsee to Kansas who later moved to Oklahoma. As late as 1916 a band of Plains Ojibwa under Chief Rocky Boy joined a group of Cree, formerly from Saskatchewan, in Montana. By all these treaties they relinquished control of their lands and its natural resources, which became, and continues to be, a contentious issue on both sides of the border. Several leaders challenged government officials to amend ambiguous treaty details, notably in Canada Chiefs Pegius and Yellow Quill, and in Wisconsin Chief Buffalo from La Pointe. They journeyed to Washington to suspend a proposed move of the Wisconsin Ojibwa to Minnesota after 400 Ojibwa had died attempting to obtain their treaty annuities at Sandy Lake, MN.

TREATIES INVOLVING THE OJIBWA OR OTHER TRIBES

WITH THE UNITED STATES
Fort McIntish 1785
Fort Harmar 1789
Greenville 1795
Fort Industry 1805
Detroit 1807
Brownstown 1808
Springwells 1815
St. Louis 1816 — Ottawa, Ojibwa, and Potawatomi
Miami Rapids 1817
St. Mary's Treaty 1818
Saginaw 1819
Sault Ste. Marie 1820
L'Arbre Croche and Michilimackinac 1820
Chicago 1821
Prairie du Chien 1825
Chicago 1833
Fond du Lac 1826
Butte des Morts 1827
Green Bay 1828
Prairie du Chien 1829
Washington 1836 — Ottawa and Chippewa
Washington 1836 — Swan Creek and Black River Bands
Detroit 1837
St. Peters 1837 — White Pine Treaty
Flint River 1837
Saganaw Treaties
 — Saganaw 1838
 — Supplemental Treaty 1839
La Pointe 1842 — Copper Treaty
 — Isle Royale Agreement 1844
Potawatomi Creek 1846
Fond du Lac 1847
Leech Lake 1847
La Pointe 1854
Washington 1855
Detroit 1855 — Ottawa and Chippewa
Detroit 1855 — Sault Ste. Marie Band
Detroit 1855 — Swan Creek and Black River
  Bands
Sac and Fox Agency 1859
Washington 1863
Old Crossing 1863
Old Crossing 1864
Washington 1864
Isabella Reservation 1864
Washington 1866
Red Lake Band of Chippewa — 1866
Washington 1867
Red Lake Band of Chippewa — 1889

WITH GREAT BRITAIN
Fort Niagara 1764
Fort Niagara 1781
Indian Officers' Land Treaty 1783
The Crawford Purchases 1783
Between the Lakes Purchases 1784
Toronto Purchase 1787
 — Indenture to the Toronto Purchase 1805
The McKee Purchase 1790
Between the Lakes Purchase 1792
Chenail Ecarte (Sombra Township) Purchase 1796
London Township Purchase 1796
Land for Joseph Brant 1797
Penetanguishene Bay Purchase 1798
St Joseph Island 1798
Head-of-the-Lake Purchase 1806
Lake Simcoe-Lake Huron Purchase 1815
Lake Simcoe-Nottawasaga Purchase 1818
Ajetance Purchase 1818
Rice Lake Purchase 1818
The Rideau Purchase 1819
Long Woods Purchase 1822
Huron Tract Purchase 1827
Saugeen Tract agreement 1836
Manitoulin Agreement 1836

The Robinson Treaties
 — Ojibwa Indians of Lake Superior 1850
 — Ojibwa Indians of Lake Huron 1850
 — Manitoulin Island Treaty 1862

WITH CANADA — BRITISH CROWN
No. 1 Stone Fort Treaty 1871 (Lower Fort Garry)
No. 2 Manitoba Post 1871
No. 3 Northwest Angle Treaty 1873
No. 4 Qu'Appelle Treaty 1874
No. 5 Berens River and Norway House 1875
No. 6 Fort Carlton 1876
(No. 7 did not involve Ojibwa)
No. 8 Gouard, Alberta 1899
No. 9 James Bay Treaty 1905–1906
No. 5 Adhesions 1908–1910
The Williams Treaties 1923
—The Chippewa Indians
—The Mississauga Indians
  Treaty No. 9 Adhesions 1929–1930

WITH FRANCE
La Grande Paix de Montréal 1701

Above: In 1844 George Henry or Maungwudaus, "a great hero" (1811–1855), a former Methodist teacher, helped organize a dance troupe to tour, consisting of his own family and some non-Christian Indians from Walpole Island. Two died from smallpox; another, George Henry's wife, died in England. Photographer unknown, from a daguerreotype c. 1848. *Indian Affairs Library and Archives Canada, e011067375*

However, the reservations were too small to maintain a traditional hunting-fishing-gathering economy and significant changes were brought by white Indian agents, miners, farmers, missionaries, and lumber companies. After 1887 U.S. federal agents sought to dispose of reservation lands unoccupied by Indian families — a process that did not end until 1934. By and large reservation populations were characterized by poverty, poor housing and an educational system that often separated the young from their traditional families and Indian values. Several reservation communities had more mixed bloods (increasingly referred to as Métis in Canada) and non status Indians always formed a sizeable section of the population on every reserve in Canada.

The final geographical range of Ojibwa bands and communities is truly impressive: from Rice Lake in eastern Ontario to Moberley Lake in British Columbia and from central Ontario to Oklahoma, it is an area greater than that occupied by any other native North American Indian people with the possible exception of the Cree. They are not really a "tribe" in a conventional sense, but their traditional patrilineal totemic clans allowed individuals, families, and small groups to move huge distances to join same-clan kinsmen to find new homes, hunting grounds, or work. Through this network they became, and still are, a people linked by history and culture.

However, the years have taken their toll on their knowledge of tribal lore, language, and arts and crafts. There are probably fewer than 25,000 Ojibwa speakers in Canada and considerably fewer within the U.S. The proportion of native speakers increases in the more northerly regions, as does adherence to old religious practices. Although there are relatively few Ojibwa free of European blood, especially French from the old fur-trade days or more recently Indians marrying non-Indians, many still bear the physical characteristics that mark them as Indian. However, the most important symbol of Ojibwa identity is the collective ownership of land, and the primary issue is dealing with government officials in a continuous struggle for survival as a people. Like all Indians, their men served in world wars and their women moved to cities for war work, and numerous families now live in urban centers away from their traditional communities. Despite recent improvements in living standards in some areas by a wealth provided by casinos and hotels on some reservations, they remain vulnerable to poverty and ill health.

In recent decades there has been a revival and renewed interest in their past. During the 1860–1870 period Saulteaux living on the Canadian prairies were introduced to a variant of the Sioux Grass Dance, a quasi-religious men's ritual that carried elements of warrior society paraphernalia. This was also introduced to the Woodland Ojibwa of Minnesota and Wisconsin in a form known as the Dream Dance or Drum Religion. Promoting friendship, it was more acceptable to white agency officials than traditional rites such as the Midewiwin. The Dream Dance and Midewiwin rituals encouraged the wearing of heavily beaded regalia by both men and women participants to emphasize their ethnicity during this period of great social change for the Ojibwa. The Dream Dance appears to be a forerunner of today's powwow, Pan-Indian celebrations held on most reservations and even in the most acculturated Ontario reserve communities. Several aspects of this phenomenon appear to be Ojibwa-inspired. Today's Ojibwa dancers wear colorful attire attesting their continued racial pride during these celebrations.

A combined census of 300,577 Ojibwa, Chippewa, Ottawa, Algonkin, and Ojibwa-Cree mixed (Canada) were reported in 2000 (U.S.) and 2006 (Canada). There were approximately 8,300 fluent native Ojibwa speakers in the U.S. and 25,000 in Canada, but only 1,000 as a first language. The Ottawa had 8,000 speakers, all but 400 in Canada.

Top: Publicity image of William F. Cody (Buffalo Bill) with former enemies, men of the Ojibwa and Sioux, together in a "Peace Council."

Above: Singers and drummers during the Dream Dance ritual at Lac du Flambeau, WI, 1933.

Chapter 2: Demography

Above and Opposite: Two members of the second group of Mississauga Ojibwa performers who crossed the Atlantic Ocean and worked with Catlin in his Indian Gallery during 1845–1846, and were painted by him. **Above** is Udjejock or Pelican, a boy (first left, front row in Catlin's cartoon, see p. 21). **Opposite** is Saysaygon or Hail Storm (fourth left, back row). Catlin no doubt provided Plains Indian regalia for their demonstrations.

SOUTHEASTERN OJIBWA OR MISSISSAUGA

These are terms which refer to Ojibwa peoples who established themselves around the northeastern rim of Lake Huron and Georgian Bay in present-day Ontario. They moved into a vacuum created by the dispersal of the sedentary Hurons and their relatives in 1649–1656 by the Iroquois, and held the area first by a successful defensive war and then, by the end of the 17th century, they had conquered the southern Ontario peninsula area.

Their ancestors were the Indians the French Jesuits met in 1640 and called *Saulteurs* or *Saulteaux* (*Bawa'tigowiniwug*) "people of the falls (Sault in French)" a reference to the falls of St. Mary at the junction of Lakes Superior and Huron. It is probable explorer Samuel de Champlain met some as early as 1615 and Brûlé met them in 1622. At the "Sault," numbers of fish-gathering Ojibwa assembled each summer and fall, and by the mid-17th century several groups had been identified in that area by the French, such as the Marameg, Noquet, and Amikwa who may have been totemic clans rather than sub-tribes. The French had established missions on Manitoulin Island by 1648 and at Sault Ste. Marie by 1655. However, by the end of the 17th century they had moved into southern Ontario and part of the lower peninsula of Michigan. The influx of the Ojibwa into these areas increased their trade with the French and British for their desirable metal goods in exchange for native procured furs, most notably beaver.

By the early 18th century the Southeastern Ojibwa had become part of a generalized Upper Great Lakes Indian Culture becoming dependent upon the exchange of fur-bearing animals for metal tools, knives, and hatchets that replaced less efficient native tools of bone and stone. Iron and copper pots were more durable than those of clay and bark, and wool clothing easier to make or obtain than those of animal skins. They had also become a significant military force when combined with Ottawa, Potawatomi, and Wyandot (reformed Hurons). They had now become economically integrated with Europeans particularly in their southern villages at Rice Lake, Saugeen, Walpole Island, and Credit in what is now southern Ontario.

These Ojibwa were generally in alliance with the French during the Anglo-French struggles and were present in the coalitions of Indian warriors aiding Langlade's destruction of Pickawillany (1752), and at Forts Duquesne, Oswego, and William Henry during the French and Indian Wars 1754–1760. They were generally supportive of the British during the American Revolution but as defeated Loyalist refugees and Iroquois flooded into Upper Canada (Ontario) 1783–1795 following the British defeat, the Ojibwa were consequently soon outnumbered in their homeland. However, they united with the Loyalist settlers and Iroquois during the War of 1812 during the American invasion of Upper Canada.

Little information is known about the Ojibwa way of life at this period, but the southernmost bands, now vastly outnumbered in their own territory, transformed from traditional subsistence on game and fish to sedentary farming. Those on the north shore of Lake Huron continued to follow traditional practices: hunting, raising corn, fishing, gathering wild rice, and tapping maple syrup. The southern bands began to cede their lands to the British Crown and American governments and many reserves in Canada were established with the aid of missionary societies after 1830. Their housing changed from traditional bark lodges to log cabins, and bark canoes to rowboats and sailboats. Some religious practices remained, but many became Christians.

By the 1930s the Southeastern Ojibwa had been largely acculturated and by the 1980s many were urbanized. The Michigan bands had moved to the Isabella Reservation and a small number moved to Kansas. The Ontario bands now numbered in excess of 50,000 registered on the First Nations reserves, with more than half in the adjacent towns and cities and much mixed with whites and, particularly, with Ottawa and Potawatomi. Recently Pan-Indian celebrations have become popular in summer months attracting many visitors.

Their reserves are: Walpole Island, Sarnia, Kettle & Stony Point, Saugeen, Chief's Point, Cape Croker, Saugeen-Cape Coker hunting reserve, Scugog, Rice Lake, Sugar Island, Alnwick, Mud Lake, Georgina Island, Rama, Christian Islands, Moose Deer Point, Parry Island, Shawanaga, Naiscoutaing, Magnetawan, Henvey Inlet, French River, Dokis, Nipissing, Wahnapitie, Whitefish Lake, Whitefish River, Spanish River, Serpent River, Mississagi River, Thessalon, Garden River, Bay Mills (U.S.), Cockburn Island, Sheshegwaning, West Bay, Sucker Creek, Sheguiandah, Wikwemikong, Caradoc, and New Credit. In recent times the Southeastern Ojibwa home became noted for their colorful porcupine quillwork on bark boxes that are sold widely and collected by museums and tourists.

SOUTHWESTERN OJIBWA OR "CHIPPEWA"

The southwestern Ojibwa, popularly known as "Chippewa" are no doubt descended from the people first described by Europeans in the Jesuit *Relation* (ecclesiastical report) of 1640 and likely met by explorers Brûlé and Nicollet before, under the name *Baouichtigovin* (probably *Bawa'tigowiniwug*) "people of the Sault." This location is where the

Nine Ojibwa Indians were brought to Europe by the Canadian promoter Arthur Rankin who joined forces with George Catlin the artist in the spring of 1843 when the artist was exhibiting his Indian Gallery in Manchester (see p. 21.) The Ojibwas were summoned to Windsor Castle to dance for Queen Victoria. In August 1844, the Ojibwas were succeeded by a group of Iowas who performed at Vauxhall Gardens and Lords Cricket Ground. These in turn were succeeded by a group of 12 Mississaugas who also visited Paris and Brussels during 1845–1846. They made a big impression on King Louis-Philippe when they performed for the royal family in Paris.

Top: O-ge-mah-o-cha-wub (Mountain Chief), Leech Lake Ojibwa, c. 1865. He wears a turban with an eagle feather, treaty medal, trade blanket, and holds a pipe and stem. Photograph: J.E.Whitney, St. Paul, MN.

Bottom: Chippewa Axel Pasey with his family, Grand Portage Band, 1936. *NARA 2128360*

Lakes Superior and Huron join at Sault Ste. Marie, although it is probable related groups occupied the north shore of Lake Huron as far east as Lake Nipissing and the eastern parts of the upper and lower peninsulas of present-day Michigan. Several sub groups are mentioned, such as the Nouquet, Marameg, Mikinac, Amikwa, and many others who may have been quasi-independent totemic clan groups that emerged throughout the early 17th century. After two centuries of expansion in the ultimately vast Ojibwa domain, these exogamic clans became no longer local, but scattered among numerous villages and bands. Clan membership was a potent factor in the integration of immigrants into new and far-distant villages. Typical clans reported by Warren and Schoolcraft in the 19th century include Bear, Beaver, Crane, and Catfish with some arranged in phratries.

During the period 1640–1670 the "Saulteaurs" who remained in the Sault Ste. Marie area accepted the Jesuits, who established an important mission. Fur trade with the French preceded the missionaries with great amounts of peltry transported to Montreal and Quebec. We know the Ojibwa and their neighbors, the Ottawa and Nipissing, conducted joint ceremonials such as the Feast of the Dead, a reburial ritual held about every 12 years, which also established and maintained alliances. These were reported in the Jesuit *Relations* of this period. It was also a period of almost constant conflict with the Iroquois who were increasingly pressing into the upper Great Lakes for new hunting grounds, particularly for beaver fur. However, the tide turned with the Ojibwa Oumisagai branch (Mississauga) reconquering the southern Ontario peninsula by the end of the century.

Hunting and trading parties spread north and west of Lake Superior, and west along the upper Michigan peninsula to Keweenaw Bay and by 1692 to Chequamegon Bay where the French had a trading post at La Pointe. The Ojibwa were able to move westward during a period of peace with the once hostile Dakota (commonly known as the Sioux), but as the French explored west, the Ojibwa themselves were obliged to attempt to expand into new areas which the Dakota had occupied for generations, hunting game, fishing, collecting wild rice, and maple sugar. They were establishing their own villages in this formerly Dakota land thus bringing the two peoples into conflicts which continued until reservations were established in the mid-19th century. From their main settlement on Madeline Island in Chequamegon Bay the Ojibwa of Lake Superior began to move inland to what is now northern Wisconsin and into the upper reaches of the Chippewa, Flambeau, and Wisconsin rivers, establishing permanent villages at Lac Courte Oreilles and Lac du Flambeau.

Linguistic and historical evidence suggest the Ojibwa were, perhaps, one people with the Ottawa and Potawatomi and as a group sided with the French during the colonial wars between France and Great Britain between 1689 and 1763. After the French and Indian War 1754–1760, France lost Canada and the Midwest to the British, but unlike the French who mixed and intermarried with the Indians, the British had a poor relationship with the native people, which led to the pan-Indian rebellion against the British known as the "Conspiracy of Pontiac" in 1763.

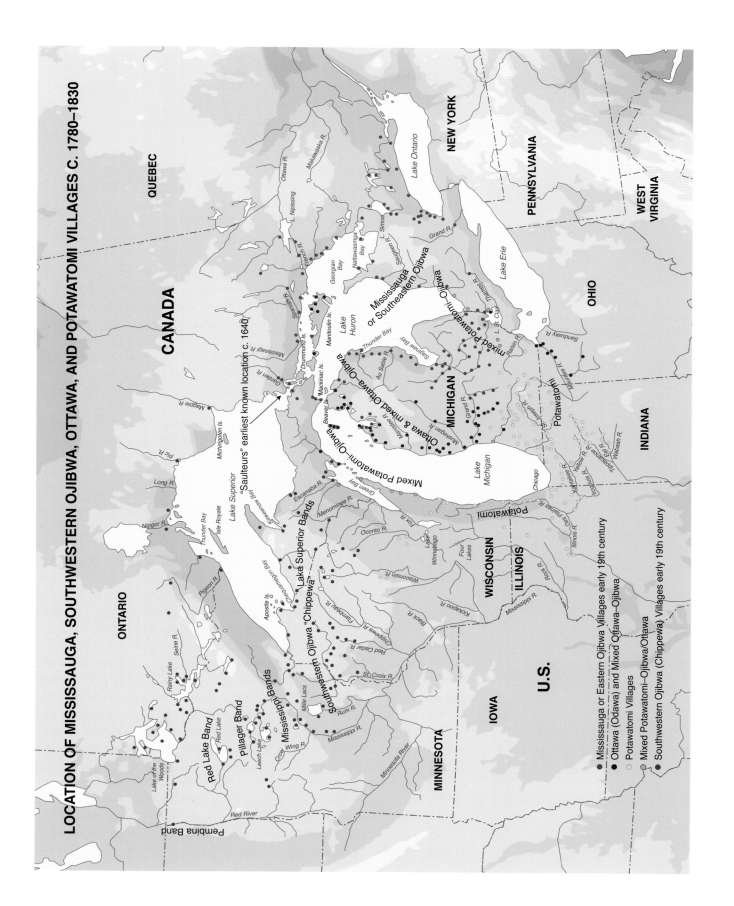

LOCATION OF MISSISSAUGA, SOUTHWESTERN OJIBWA, OTTAWA, AND POTAWATOMI VILLAGES C. 1780–1830

Above: Wa-em-boesh-kaa, *A Chippewa Chief*, by Charles Bird King or Henry Inman, from the original painting by James Otto Lewis at the Treaty of Fond du Lac in 1826. He was one of at least six members of the Sandy Lake Ojibwa who signed the treaty. He holds a pipe and wears a headdress of duck and woodpecker feathers. See McKenney and Hall Vol. 1.

Below: Little Shell, Ojibwa (Chippewa), 1874. The photograph was probably taken during a visit to Washington, D.C. He wears a treaty or "Peace medal" and a neckband of cloth with floral beadwork.

Although eastern bands of Ojibwa took part, French traders in northern Wisconsin urged the Ojibwa in that area not to join the rebellion. After the revolt was suppressed the British took a more conciliatory approach to the Ojibwa of Wisconsin, who later became their staunch allies after the American Revolution ended in 1783 with the Treaty of Paris.

The Ojibwa took little part in the war in the Ohio Country when the Indian coalition of Miamis, Potawatomis, and others under the leadership of Little Turtle defeated the Americans under Harmar and later St. Clair, which was finally ended by General Wayne at Fallen Timbers in 1794. However, British influence continued in the Great Lakes region through their trading companies such as the North West Company operating trading posts in Ojibwa territory in northern Wisconsin and Minnesota until 1815 at the close of the War of 1812. In 1805–1806 an American Army officer, Zebulon Pike, attempted to undermine the British influence and still present French-Canadian traders when he led an expedition up the Mississippi River to parley with the Indians, but this had little effect as the Ojibwa believed the U.S. was only interested in annexation. Consequently, some became adherents of the Shawnee Prophet (Tenskwatawa) and his brother Tecumseh. The Ojibwa in the Detroit area fought with Tecumseh against the Americans during the War of 1812, although Ojibwa bands from Wisconsin and Minnesota stayed out of the fighting despite being pro-British.

After the close of the war the Americans intensified efforts to end the conflict between the Ojibwa and Dakota by the Prairie du Chien Treaty of 1825, and at Fond du Lac, Minnesota in 1826. By ending the intertribal fighting the Americans hoped to pressure the Indians to sell their lands. The eastern bands in Michigan had begun to cede their lands in 1807, 1819, and 1836, although the bands of Saginaw, Swan Creek, and Black River did not obtain their Isabella Reservation until 1855–1864; a few actually moved to Kansas. Between 1820 and 1836 the eastern part of the upper Michigan peninsula was ceded (with the Ottawa ceding the western part of the lower peninsula). The government then made two major land cession treaties with the Lake Superior Ojibwa in 1837 and in 1842–1848 for lands in the western half of the upper Michigan peninsula, north-central Wisconsin, and eastern Minnesota. American settlers soon exploited the rich pine stands and copper mines along the southern shore of Lake Superior. The government of Zachary Taylor hoped to move the northern Wisconsin bands to Minnesota but after a delegation of chiefs visited Washington, the next president, Millord Fillmore, agreed to new treaties beginning in 1854–1866 for the remaining Superior bands to stay in Wisconsin, and the Mississippi and Pillager bands to have reservations in Minnesota, excluding the Red Lake bands who were treated separately by the U.S. government in 1889. Some issues resulting from these treaties and the reservation lands created have never been satisfactorily resolved.

After the reservations were established the Ojibwa were unable to sustain themselves by traditional hunting and gathering because of the reduced land base. The white-owned lumber companies provided some employment and economic benefits but also encouraged land sales. In 1887 Congress passed the Dawes Act by which most of the reservations were

SOUTHWESTERN OJIBWA BANDS RECOGNIZED BY TREATIES

The following were recognized by treaties with the U.S. government in the 19th century.

Lake Superior Chippewa Bands
L'Anse ⎤
Ontonagon ⎦ Keweenaw Bay Band

Lac Vieux Desert*

Red Cliff ⎤
Bad River ⎦ La Pointe Band

Lac Courte Oreilles
Lac du Flambeau
St. Croix
Sokaogon (Mole Lake)
Fond du Lac
Grand Portage

*separated from Keweenaw
Bay in 1988

Mississippi River Chippewa Bands
Crow Wing
Gull Lake
Pelican Lake
Pokegama Lake
Rabbit Lake
Rice Lake
Sandy Lake
Swan River
Trout Lake
White Oak Point

Pillager Chippewa Bands
Lake Winnibigoshish
Leech Lake
Otter Tail Lake (White Earth)
Pillager
Cass Lake

Pembina Chippewa Bands
White Earth (part)
Red Lake (part)
Little Shell (Montana and
    North Dakota)
Chippewa Cree (Montana)
Roseau River (Manitoba)
Turtle Mt. (North Dakota)

Red Lake Chippewa Band
Treated separately by the
U.S. government.

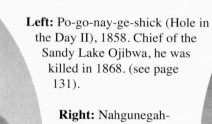

Left: Po-go-nay-ge-shick (Hole in the Day II), 1858. Chief of the Sandy Lake Ojibwa, he was killed in 1868. (see page 131).

Right: Nahgunegah-bow (Standing Forward) chief of the Rabbit Lake "Chippewa," c. 1872. The Mississippi River Ojibwa bands were assigned six reservations in Minnesota by 1867, five of which were never effectively established: Sandy Lake, Gull Lake, Rabbit Lake, Pokegama, and White Oak Point. Their status remains an issue.

divided up into individual family sections for farming. However, the land in northern Wisconsin and Minnesota was not good for farming, so to supplement their wages many Ojibwa sold or leased their land to lumber companies so that over 90% of reservation land by the 1930s had passed into white control. However, Red Lake remained unallotted.

In 1934 the Indian Reorganization Act during the Franklin D. Roosevelt administration halted the sale of Indian lands and new reservations and band communities were created at Mole Lake, WI, in 1937 and St. Croix, WI, in 1938, and Grand Traverse, MI, in 1984. Throughout much of the 20th century Ojibwa communities were characterized by poverty, poor health, and unemployment. World War I and II saw many men serve in the armed services and many families moved to the cities to find war work and many never returned to the reservations.

The Ojibwas' special attachment to their lands was enhanced in 1983 when their treaty rights to hunt and fish on lands they had ceded to the U.S. in 1837 and 1842 was upheld by the federal courts despite many unsuccessful attempts to reverse the decision. Increased control of their own affairs and social programs have seen a marked improvement in health and housing on many reservations together with huge incomes from casinos and hotels by the beginning of the 21st century.

The Ojibwa survived the impact of the white man's culture for a time more successfully than any other Indian people in the Upper Great Lakes region, suffering less from the colonial and revolutionary wars and diseases in some areas. Their main enemy was the Dakota (Eastern Sioux) who maintained a trade and hunting network in the St. Croix River area and other major Mississippi River tributaries. With the arrival of Ojibwa from their cultural center in La Pointe the area became a contested place. However, with the Treaty of Prairie du Chien of 1825 the U.S. attempted to draw boundaries separating the Ojibwa and Dakota and a number of Dakota were adopted as Ojibwa in the Wolf totem. Throughout the 18th century the Ojibwa had spread out from La Pointe into lands conquered from the Dakota people, and settled into several village sites. These bands in the western Lake Superior and Mississippi River regions regarded La Pointe as their "capital" and center for trade and spirituality.

For simplicity the text, maps, and reserve/reservations lists have separated the Southwestern and Northern Ojibwa at the U.S./Canadian border, although the Lake of the Woods and Rainy River bands in Ontario are culturally closer to the Minnesota Ojibwa than the Northern Ojibwa.

Above: Ju-Ah-Kis-Gaw, an Ojibwa woman with a child in cradle, wearing a cloth strap dress. Painting by George Catlin, c. 1834, at Fort Snelling, MN.

Opposite: The Ojibwa, Ottawa (Odawa), and Potawatomi reservations, lands, bands, and communities in the United States' Great Lakes region.

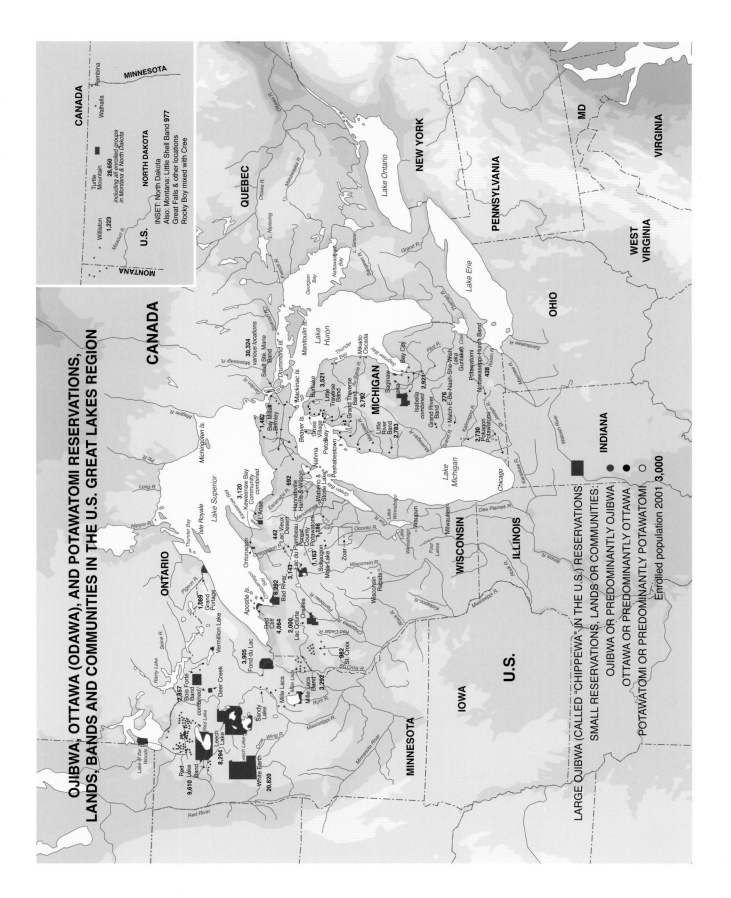

OJIBWA, OTTAWA (ODAWA), AND POTAWATOMI RESERVATIONS,
LANDS, BANDS AND COMMUNITIES IN THE U.S. GREAT LAKES REGION

Right: "Chippewa Cree," dance troupe, Rocky Boy Reservation, MT, c. 1940.

Below: Shingwaukonse or Shingwaskonce (Little Pine) 1773–1854. Important Ojibwa chief from the Canadian side of the Great Lakes. Fought for the British in the War of 1812 but later involved with repairing relations with the Americans. His son George Shingwauk (1839–1920) successfully managed the affairs and promoted religious harmony among the Anglican and Catholic Ojibwa of the Garden River band, many of whom had been forcibly moved by settlers from Sault St. Marie. After a drawing by Martin Somerville, Montreal, c. 1840.

NORTHERN OJIBWA AND SAULTEAUX

There were relatively few Ojibwa north of Lake Superior until the late 17th century when the Hudson's Bay Company began to build trading posts on the coast of Hudson and James bays to accommodate the Cree and Assiniboine. As a result the French established posts at Thunder Bay (1678), Lake Nipigon (1684), and at the junction of the Kenogami and Albany rivers (1685). The competition between the British and French was creating hostilities between the Cree and Ojibwa who had encroached into Cree domains. As a result the Cree gradually moved north and west from the Shield country north of Lake Superior. They were gradually replaced by the Ojibwa expanding north and occupying lands vacated by the Cree. By the 1740s some Ojibwa were trading at the coastal Hudson's Bay Company posts but most continued to trade with the French. Some were already as far north as the Ogoki River and west to Lac Seul and Lake of the Woods pushing the Cree and Assiniboine farther west. By the 1760s following the French defeat at Quebec, large bands of emergent northern Ojibwa were traveling to Fort Albany and Moose Factory to trade with the British.

About this period some Ojibwa and some Ottawa expanded further northwest towards Island and Gods' Lakes where Fort Severn and York Factory Hudson's Bay Company posts traded with them. Also, Ojibwa from the south shore of Lake Superior were establishing residency on the

Above: Saulteaux Indians, Fort Garry, Manitoba, c. 1857–1858, by William Napier. *Library and Archives Canada 3007530*

Opposite, Below right: Eagleman "Chippewa Cree," Rocky Boy Reservation, Montana c. 1930s. By 1916 a number of Plains Ojibwa people from several reservations including the Coeur d'Alene, Flathead, Crow, and Blackfeet reservations settled on the new Rocky Boy Reservation, although a number also settled near Great Falls, a location called Hill 57. Others remained "land-less" with a continuing grievance against the U.S. government. The Cree and Ojibwa of western Montana had adopted the buck-skin and beadwork attire of the Blackfeet and Assiniboine for their dress-up occasions by this period.

Above: Charlie Assiniboine (d. 1924) and his brother, Canadian Saulteaux. Both wear typical cloth leggings with beadwork decoration and bandolier bags. They were from the Portage Band, Manitoba.

Opposite, Above: Two Ottawa (Odawa) chiefs from Michilimackinac and Lake Huron, painting by Sir Joshua Jebb. Both chiefs wear silver brooches, medals, and earrings. The man on the left wears a trade cloth coat and the chief on the right wears a painted skin robe. *Library and Archives, Canada.*

Opposite, Below: Male and Female, Ottawas, 1801. *Library and Archives, Canada.*

east side of Lake Winnipeg. Even today there is a dialectic difference between the Ojibwa spoken on the east shore of Lake Winnipeg and the dialect spoken in the Severn River drainage. The Midewiwin ceremony is also part of the traditions of the former area but absent among the Northern Ojibwa in their eastern sectors until borrowed during the 19th century. The Ojibwa groups who came to occupy the area north and west of Lake Superior during the second half of the 18th century were large in size and highly mobile, trading with the Hudson's Bay Company and joining their southern relatives in wars with the Dakota. Evidence indicates their environment was capable of supporting large bands with plentiful moose, caribou, and beaver. By the early 1780s the Hudson's Bay Company's monopoly of the fur trade was challenged by the formation of the famous North West Company by Montreal merchants who also established posts north of Lake Superior. This competition forced the Hudson's Bay Company to establish a series of inland posts to trade with the Northern Ojibwa who continued to move westward. By the time of the amalgamation of the Hudson's Bay and North West companies in 1821 they were well established in the vicinity of Lake Winnipeg.

Their harsh environment precluded any horticulture and many bands were outside the range of wild rice and maple sugar. The abundance of trade goods gradually brought changes to their material culture. Moose and caribou provided clothing for mens' tunics and womens' dresses. Some mens' coats, possibly influenced by traders' uniforms, highly decorated with painted designs and quillwork, have survived in museums' collections, and several types of native objects have continued in use until recent times, such as snowshoes, cradleboards, moccasins, and canoes. Winter transport equipment includes toboggans and canoe-sleds, and large dogs were acquired around the 1780s to pull them. The decline in native material culture was reflected in the emergence of large permanent native settlements of Euro-Canadian structures replacing native wigwams. The Northern Ojibwa did not experience the settlement problems faced by their southern and southeastern relatives and were able to adjust their life styles and retain aspects of their sociopolitical organizations, hunting groups, kinship patterns, and language in their subarctic environment.

The Canadian government (the Crown) began signing treaties with the Northern Ojibwa, recognizing permanent bands beginning in 1850 on the north shore of Lake Superior. There were treaties at Lac Seul, 1873; Osnaburg, Fort Hope, Martin Falls, 1906; Island Lake, 1909; Deer Lake, 1910; and Trout and Caribou Lakes, 1929–1930. Cultural changes increased with the construction of the Canadian Pacific Railway in the 1880s and by the 1930s airplanes were flying-in supplies to remote regions. As road construction reached north, the Northern Ojibwa adjusted to the Canadian industrial economy.

The so-called Saulteaux of the Lake Winnipeg area, who had closest contact with the newly arriving European settlers in the early 19th century, denied the Lord Selkirk Treaty on the grounds it was signed by so-called chiefs they did not recognize. A Crown Commissioner was appointed and Treaty No. 1 was signed in 1871 and Treaty No. 3 in 1873. The principal features were the relinquishment of their lands for reserves and for the provision of schools, prohibition of the sale of liquor, and payment of annuities. Treaty No. 3 also included the north-ern bands of Lac Seul and Pikangikum. For these isolat-ed Ojibwa communities the treaties were beneficial as they lost nothing of value and instead gained recogni-tion from the government. In these isolated communi-ties trapping animals for fur and game supply remained a significant part of native life well into the second half of the 20th century. Fishing also remained a reliable source of food. Changing economic conditions, pres-sures on natural resources, and closure of commercial posts in the north, have left a number of native bands with increased populations yet poor economic and social circumstances. The distribution of government money for social housing, schools, and other projects has resulted in some allegations of corruption by some band leaders. In northern Ontario in recent times the Northern Ojibwa and Cree have intermarried and combined in several bands such as Deer Lake, Trout Lake, Caribou Lake and are often known as Oj-Cree, Cree-Chip or Severn Ojibwa. At least 30,000 people are reported.

OTTAWA (ODAWA)

These are a large group of Algonkian-speaking people whose language was so close to Ojibwa that they have often been considered as one "Anishinabe." They occu-pied both shores of Lake Huron, particularly Manitoulin Island, and also parts of the lower Michigan peninsula, which they shared with some of the Potawatomi and Ojibwa. When first met by Champlain in 1615 they were near the French River, Ontario, on the canoe route between the Ottawa River and Georgian Bay. Their name is said to signify "traders." Their culture and clan structure was much the same as the Ojibwa with some horticulture similar to the Hurons. How-ever, they were quickly drawn into the fur trade and a long association with the French, and as a result were forced west due to the Iroquois aggression in their quest to gain control of valuable trade goods for peltry. During the 17th century the Ottawa sought ref-uge in various locations — Green Bay, Chequamegon Bay, and Keweenaw Bay — but gradually recovered their main habitat by the end of the century as Iroquois threats diminished. In their alliance with the Ojibwa and Potawatomi — the Three Fires — they were allied to the French in the French and Indian War, and the rebellion against the British under Pontiac in 1763.

Above: Roadside image at Burt Lake, MI, of Andrew J. Blackbird, an Ottawa leader (see p. 130).

Opposite, Above: Elderly Potawatomi woman of the Wisconsin Rapids Band near Arpin, WI, 1913. Note bark wigwam in background.

Opposite, Center: Siobhan Marks, Ojibwa, and Neil Oppendike during a celebration at the Hannahville Potawatomi in Upper Michigan. The name Potawatomi is often cited to mean "people of the place of the fire." Recently, linguists have cast doubt upon this as there is no connection with *skote* (fire) in the Potawatomi tongue. Perhaps the traditional folk etymology refers to "chosen people" or "leading tribe" with their own council fire within the Three Fires Confederacy. *Kevin Harris*

Opposite, Below: Potawatomi Indians, Athens, MI, c. 1910. The Nottawaseppi Huron band of Potawatomi (formerly called Potawatomi of Huron) are located in Calhoun County in southern Michigan, south of Battle Creek.

Later they fought for Great Britain in the Revolutionary War and the War of 1812.

As settlers flooded into Michigan they were forced to cede their lands to the U.S. during the period 1807–1837, and again in 1855. Resulting land claims had only recently been partially agreed by 1980 with some federal recognition. Three bands from Ohio, including the Blanchard's Fork and Roche de Boeuf, were granted a reservation in Franklin County, KS, in 1831 from where most moved to Ottawa County, OK, in 1868. Here an acculturated group of descendants remain on their old allotted reservation, although many have now left the area. Those who remained in Michigan are the Grand Traverse Band, centered in the Peshawbestown area, the Little River Band around Manistee, the Little Traverse Bay Band near Cross Village, Harbor Springs, L'Arbre Croche, and Petoskey. Other groups are located at Burt Lake, Mikado, Oscoda, and Grand River. The Canadian Ottawa reserves are shared with the Ojibwa, formalized by the treaties of 1850, but they are only likely to be the major part of the registered population at Wikwemikong (unceded part of Manitoulin Island), Cockburn Island, and perhaps Walpole Island. The total Ottawa population in the U.S. was given as 3,533 in 1970, and 7,975 in the U.S. 2010 census; of these, 2,290 were enrolled in Oklahoma in 2000. It is estimated that, when combined as mixed Ottawa-Ojibwa for both the U.S. and Ontario, a present population of 15,000 is probable, of which perhaps 5,000 are Ottawa alone, with about 500 native speakers. In Canada they are no longer reported separately.

The Ottawas have long been the producers of fine porcupine-quilled barkwork, baskets, model canoes, and other objects produced for sale, which have been collected by generations of curio hunters and museums.

POTAWATOMI

Potawatomi is also spelled Potawatomie or Pottawatomie, and they are also known as Fire People or People of the Place of Fire, terms which have confused origins. They often call themselves *Neshnabek* (people).

The original homeland of the Potawatomi people was the eastern shore of Lake Michigan from the St. Joseph River north to about Grand Traverse, but concentrated below the Grand River. A later location, a refuge area, was in northeastern Wisconsin, the Door Peninsula above Manitowoc, by about 1670. Once the threat of Iroquois attacks reduced, the Potawatomi cemented an alliance with New France and began a period of expansion — a process which did not finish until the end of the War of 1812 when the widely scattered Potawatomi came up against the rapidly expanding American frontier. The tribal estate by 1820 consisted of villages on either side of Lake Michigan, or rivers draining into that lake, and on the Illinois and Wabash rivers, ranging from central Wisconsin to the Detroit area. This land was not exclusively occupied by Potawatomi; in many areas villages were combined with Odawa (Ottawa) and Ojibwa. Other locations were shared with Kickapoo, Sauk, and Menominee. This range was 400 miles wide and their population at least 9,000. Before the Potawatomi were forced west during the 19th century they had been concentrated along various rivers in their homelands and are particularly associated with the Illinois, Des Plaines, and Fox rivers, IL; the Kankakee, Yellow, Tippecanoe and Wabash rivers, IN; and the St. Joseph and Elkhart rivers, MI.

In the decades after the War of 1812, as the threat of British intervention in the upper Great Lakes diminished, the Americans no longer placated the Indian tribes on their exposed frontiers. The tribes of the old Northwest Territory (mainly allies of the British in the late war) were gradually forced to agree to moves west. Several features of Potawatomi culture are particularly relevant at this period. Some Potawatomi in the Michigan-Indiana area had been subjected to religious, economic, and subsistence acculturation for generations with considerable intermarriage with French and British fur traders and military personnel. Between 1816 and 1839 the Potawatomi were induced to cede their territory to the U.S. The acculturated bands from southern Michigan and northern Indiana were the first affected and had moved to Kansas by 1841. The more conservative Wisconsin-Illinois Potawatomi moved first to Iowa then joined their relatives in Kansas in 1847. There they became known as the Prairie Band Potawatomi. The two groups did not merge, the acculturated band moved on to Oklahoma (then Indian Territory) in 1867 to be known henceforth as the Citizens' Band Potawatomi.

However, not all of them moved west. Three small groups remained in southern Michigan — the Pokagon, Huron, and Gun Lake bands — and some conservative groups sought refuge in northern Wisconsin and northern Michigan, and at least 2,000 moved across to Upper Canada where they sought a better future in the land of their former allies, the British. They were reported to have merged with the Ojibwa and Ottawa (Odawa) in almost 30 locations around the eastern rim of Lake Huron, Georgian Bay, and St. Clair River — the largest groups at Walpole Island, Kettle Point, Cape Croker, Christian Island, Parry Sound, and Manitoulin Island. Those in the U.S. were located at Stone Lake and Wabano to become the Forest County Potawatomi, also at Wisconsin Rapids, WI, and the Hannahville Community in Upper Michigan. Two small groups merged with the Menominee in Wisconsin and Kickapoo in Kansas on their respective reservations.

The year 2000 census reported 15,817 Potawatomi alone in the U.S. The BIA (Bureau of Indian Affairs) for 2001 returned 1,186 Forest Co., 692 Hannahville, 428 Huron, 2,730 Pokagon, 276 Gun Lake, 4,870 Prairie Band, and Citizen 23,557, although the blood quantum for membership was very low. In Canada none were returned separately in 2001 except 290 "Caldwell band," a mixed group

Above: Photograph of Turtle Mountain Plains Ojibwa taken about 1898. Rear row, left to right: Iron Bear, Hunts Thunder. Center row, L–R, Standing Elk, Yellow Bird, Cuts Heart, Old Face. Front row, L–R, A.C.J. Farrel, Sage Hen. Note the British military jacket worn by Hunts Thunder, the fine beaded shirt worn by Standing Elk, and the double-bowl pipe carried by Cuts Heart. *Photograph courtesy North Dakota State Historical Society.*

originally from Point Pelee claiming Potawatomi and British military person- nel ancestry (but more likely Ojibwa), scattered in southern Ontario and the Detroit area. The 2010 census showed 18,329 Potawatomi in the U.S. The Kansas Prairie band continued to maintain their clan organization and their rites including naming ceremonies and feasts until the 1930s.

NIPISSING

Sometimes considered a separate group or sub tribe of the Anishinabe group — Ojibwa, Ottawa, and Potawatomi — they lived on Lake Nipissing, Ontario, a key canoe route from Montreal via the Ottawa River and then the French River to Georgian Bay. Known to the French by 1613, the Nipissing fled to Lake Nipigon during the Iroquois wars but had returned to their lake by 1671, a route which became important for the fur trade. Later a number joined the French clergy and Mohawks at Oka. The Nipiss- ing and Dokis bands signed the Robinson-Huron Treaty of 1850 which established their reserves and a switch from fur trading to the lumber business; however, their connection to the old Nipissings is unclear.

PLAINS OJIBWA, BUNGI OR WESTERN SAULTEAUX

These are different names for Ojibwa bands who, during the late 18th century, moved west beyond the Red River of the North in present-day Manitoba into a radically different environment to their Woodlands home- land. The Red River rises near Lake Traverse on the Minnesota–South Dakota border and flows north to Lake Winnipeg, roughly marking the divide between the Woodlands and Parklands regions: the Parklands being the eastern margin of the Prairies and High Plains. Although the degree of transformation from a Forest to a Parklands culture is a matter of debate among ethnologists, there's no doubt some bands of these western Ojibwa successfully adapted in varying degrees to life in the Parkland- Prairie environment.

During the late decades of the 18th century the Ojibwa advanced west from Grand Portage through the Rainy Lake region to Lake of the Woods in search of new hunting grounds for fur-bearing animals, particularly beaver, to satisfy the demands of the North West and Hudson's Bay companies. One of the first references to Ojiwa villages in the Rainy Lake area was by Alexander Henry in 1775; this area was traditionally home to some Cree and Assiniboine. However, white traders also brought smallpox in 1780–1782 which probably hastened the Ojibwa's western move and, as a consequence, a reduction in fur-trade activity. The smallpox outbreaks affected the Cree and Assiniboine of the area more than the Ojibwa, who subsequently became the dominant people around the Lake of the Woods and Souris River regions. The west now offered some western Ojibwa bands a chance of a promising future in this new location. Another reason for the diversification of some of the western Ojibwa's hunting patterns was the disappearance of the region's beaver population due to disease.

Left: White Cloud, Chippewa (Ojibwa), Chief of the Gull Lake band, White Earth Reservation, MN, c. 1865. He wears a trade blanket. Eagle and turkey feathers decorate his hair and his painted face probably indicates his warrior status. Photograph published by Whitney & Zimmerman, St. Paul, MN.

Right: Quiwizhenshish (Bad Boy), Ojibwa, c. 1872. The arrangement of the feathers in his hair indicates his status as a warrior.

Below Left: Maw-je-ke-jik (Mah-we-do-ke-shick), Flying Sky or Spirit of the Skies, Chief of the Cass Lake Ojibwa, c. 1865. He is wearing a trade blanket-coat, probably a Hudson's Bay blanket, and holds a pipe bowl in his left hand.

Below Right: To Keep the Net Up, Chippewa (Ojibwa), from Leech Lake Reservation, MN, c. 1865. He wears a braided yarn sash across his shoulder. His coat appears to be made from a trade blanket. Photograph published by Whitney & Zimmerman, St. Paul, MN.

This encouraged some bands to join the Plains Cree and Assiniboine on winter buffalo hunts, whereas others continued to return to the Parklands and Woodlands for fishing and gathering wild rice in the fall.

The Plains Ojibwa adopted various cultural traits from their Plains Cree and Assiniboine allies. They obtained horses (although were never horse rich) and employed the buffalo-skin tipi, which replaced the birchbark and cattail mat-covered wigwams of their Woodland cousins. They adopted horse-drawn travois, rawhide parfleches, some Plains-style animal skin attire such as mens' shirts and leggings and womens' three-elk skin dresses. Moccasin types included the one-piece center-seam, the multi-piece vamp type, and the Plains separate-sole type. The marginal Parklands people utilized a fitted moosehide coat for men and strap dresses for women. Leggings for both sexes were often trade cloth. Both the Plains Ojibwa and those in the marginal zones between the Prairie, Parkland, and forest regions traded with whites for materials which gave them the benefits of European technology such as metal goods and guns. Traders also provided reflective objects that had connotations of sacred power for personal decoration such as glass beads, mirrors, colored trade cloth, and silver ornaments.

Rituals were adopted from the Plains Cree and Assiniboine, notably the rain-making Sun Dance, which ensured the return each year of the buffalo, also warrior societies: Windigokan (Clown's Society), Big Dog's Society, Buffalo Dance, and later the Grass Dance Society (probably adopted from their old enemies the Dakota or Eastern Sioux). However, the marginal groups retained the Midewiwin (Medicine Lodge) and Wabeno (Shaking Tent Ritual) societies and the belief in an all-powerful single deity.

By 1800 many had adjusted to a pattern of seasonal moves, hunting in the west but returning to the traditional villages at Red, Leech, and Rainy lakes. They also traded at posts on both the east and west sides of Lake Winnipeg and in the Interlake region between Lakes Winnipeg and Winnipegosis. They spread out across a huge territory from Fort Alexander south to Turtle Mountain, through the Interlake region along the Assiniboine, Shell, Dauphin, and Red Deer rivers, and along the North Saskatchewan to the foothills of the Rockies. Beaver remained their most important quarry for their trading economy.

In 1817, together with some Cree and Assiniboine, they ceded land along the Red and Assiniboine rivers to the Selkirk Colony in Assiniboia, an area in present-day southwest Manitoba and adjacent areas of Saskatchewan and Minnesota created by the Hudson's Bay Company (claimants to much of western Canada). Their territory was a vast area now extending south to the Turtle Mountains of North Dakota and to the eastern edge of Cypress Hills, sharing this region with Cree, Assiniboine, and Métis with whom they were now much mixed. In 1863 the Pembina Ojibwa made their first ratified treaty with the U.S., ceding portions of their easternmost territory, but until the early 1870s the majority were not covered by this or any other treaty and remained outside the jurisdiction of both the U.S. and Canada.

In Canada under treaties No. 1 (1871) and No. 2 (1873) they ceded their lands to the British Crown and accepted reserves in southern Manitoba in the Portage La Prairie and Swan Lake districts. However, for many whose territorial range was within the U.S., they continued to base their livelihood on buffalo hunting until the final collapse of the northern herds in the late 1870s. A reservation was established in the Turtle Mountains in 1882 that became home for some Plains Ojibwa and a considerable number of Métis, but many remained "landless," living or intermarried on several reservations and communities in North Dakota and Montana, such as Little Shell's Band, who spent time in both Montana and Canada. Under treaties No. 4 (1874) and No. 6 (1876) the Plains Ojibwa surrendered their lands in Saskatchewan to the British Crown and settled on reserves with numbers of Cree, Assiniboine, and Métis.

Throughout the late 19th and 20th centuries the Plains Ojibwa have gradually been forced to abandon, to a large extent, their former way of life. Most men found seasonal employment as farm workers or construction workers, but chronic unemployment characterized most communities on both sides of the border. Their men served in both world wars and other conflicts. Many relocated to towns and cities, and today fewer than half of those enrolled (U.S.) or registered (Canada) as Indian, or as members of First Nations bands, live permanently on their reservations. Recent improvements have coincided with cultural revivals, and the spread of Pan-Indian events such as powwows. They have continued to hold sun dances on several reserves.

One band of Plains Ojibwa joined the Plains Cree on the Rocky Boy Reservation in western Montana (Rocky Boy was Ojibwa), but Little Shell's Band still remains landless in Montana. There are also Ojibwa among the Cree at John O'Chiese, Alberta, and in British Columbia in the Moberley Lake district.

They also excel in the art of beadwork decoration for their native attire in geometric and floral designs, and are well represented in museum collections. Their present-day groups are shown in the table on page 44.

In considering the figures one should note the differing legal criteria employed in Canada and the United States for enrolling an individual as an Indian. Many Métis or mix blood individuals enrolled as Indian in the United States would not be so enrolled in Canada, since their ancestors may not have had Treaty Indian status. This factor accounts for the rather large Plains Ojibwa population listed for the Turtle Mountain Reservation in North Dakota, and for the Trenton and Walhalla non reservation communities in their entirety. About a half of each of the populations listed are living off the reserves/reservations. The Plains Ojibwa tribe by 1972 had almost doubled in numbers since 1958, the first date for which we have accurate data.

It should be recognized that dividing the Ojibwa into these various regional divisions is fairly arbitrary, in particular for the Plains Ojibwa. Several bands were only marginal to the Plains. One Saskatchewan band, the Key, population 1,114 in 2005, should probably be included in the Plains Ojibwa section as well. A number of Plains and Woods Cree bands also have Ojibwa ancestry, such as the Waterhen Lake band.

Above: Plains Ojibwa man from Long Plains Reserve, southern Manitoba, 1896. His cloth shirt with beaded strips, roundels, and elaborate neckband is typical of a number of similar examples from Long Plains and Turtle Mountain ND.

Opposite, Above: Saulteaux camp at Lake St. Martin, Manitoba, 1888.

Opposite, Below: Plains Ojibwa man from the Long Plains Reserve, c. 1900 in Manitoba. He wears a typical shirt with large beaded disks on the front. He also holds a floral beaded octopus bag.

PLAINS OJIBWA PRESENT-DAY GROUPS

UNITED STATES

Name	Population 1972	2001	Nearby town or city
NORTH DAKOTA			
Turtle Mountain Reservation	16,000	28,650*	Dunseith, Belcourt, and Rolla
Trenton community	400	1,223	Williston
Walhalla community	400	?	Walhalla

* includes Métis communities in N. Dakota and Montana.

MONTANA			
Rocky Boy Reservation*	1,700	5,728	Havre
Little Shell's Band (still seeking federal status)			landless

* mixed with Plains-Cree and now entirely Cree linguistically. Plains-Ojibwa made up about one third of the original group.

CANADA

Name	Population 1972	2005	Nearby town or city
MANITOBA			
Gambler	28	149	McCauley
Keeseekoowenin	316	992	Elphinstone
Long Plain	839	3,362	Portage La Prairie
Peguis	2,230	7,846	Dallas
Rolling River	325	893	Erickson
Roseau River	783	2,069	Letellier
Sandy Bay	1,516	5,164	Amaranth
Swan Lake	463	1,166	Swan Lake
Waywayseecappo	757	2,204	Birdtail
SASKATCHEWAN			
Coté	1,516	2,932	Kamsack
Fishing Lake	488	1,477	Wadena
Kahkewistahaw	498	1,548	Broadview
Keeseekcose	686	2,006	Pelly
Knistin(o)	309	827	Rose Valley
Muscowequan	491	1,434	Lestock
Muscowpetung	430	1,119	Edenwold
Nut Lake or Yellow Quill	864	2,455	Rose Valley
Ochapowace	458	1,410	Broadview
Pasqua	523	1,665	Ft. Qu'Appelle
Sakimay &Shesheep	524	1,357	Broadview
Saulteaux	360	1,090	Cochin
White Bear mixed with Plains-Cree and	958	2,165	Carlyle
Assiniboine (Plains-Ojibwa about 1/3 of total)			
Approximate total population	31,729	80,000	

MÉTIS

This term has a number of meanings for people of mixed European and native ancestry. The name is derived from the Latin term *mixticius*. In North America the French term Métis is employed, or Mestizo in Latin America. In its strictest meaning it was once limited to people of French and Indian genealogy who formed settlements at the Red River of the North's junction with the Assiniboine River in present-day Manitoba. However, in its wider sense the term Métis has been increasingly applied and adopted by people of mixed European and native descent, especially in northern and western Canada, whose forebears may have had no connection with the Red River Métis. However, for various reasons, they were excluded from registration as Indians in the treaties between the native people and the British Crown, and denied enrollment in the U.S. where they have been regarded as Canadian nationals.

The origins of the Métis were the natural outcome of the North American fur trade where Europeans (particularly French and British) took native wives. The foundations for the settlement of the Great Lakes by French-Canadian fur traders followed the explorations of the second half of the 17th century and by the mid-18th century there were perhaps 50 major mixed-blood communities in the region ranging from Detroit, Kaskaskia, and Michilimackinac. Subsequently, this region passed from French control to the British, then Americans, which together with the diminishing fur returns, resulted in the mixed bloods rejoining their native communities, or absorbed into the growing white communities, or they found their way to the Red River area of present-day Manitoba, where many were employed by the newly formed North West Company towards the end of the 18th century. These Métis were in direct competition with the older Hudson's Bay Company, founded in 1670, whose traders worked west and south from Hudson's and James bays through a vast region claimed by the British and called Rupert's Land. Many of the mixed bloods of the Hudson's Bay Company were of Cree origin, those of the North West Company, whose French ancestors came originally from Lower Canada, were of Ojibwa and Ottawa extraction and largely Roman Catholic. In 1811, in order to maintain preeminence in the fur trade, the Hudson's Bay Company (claimants to much of western Canada) gave jurisdiction of an area of present-day southwest Manitoba and adjacent areas of Saskatchewan and Minnesota to Thomas Selkirk, 5th Earl of Selkirk, an area known as Assinibonia. He recruited Scottish and Swiss colonists. In 1816 a confrontation took place at Seven Oaks between the two fur trade companies and their respective personnel and mixed bloods that was only resolved when the companies merged in 1821. Fur traders and redundant employees and from both companies had produced two

Below: The fight between the North West Company, Métis, and Indians, with the Selkirk settlers and Hudson's Bay Company traders at Seven Oaks on the Red River in 1816. Painting by C.W. Jeffreys.

separate populations — the English and Scottish traders and their part-native descendants and Indian wives, mostly Protestant from the area of Rupert's Land; and the French-speaking Métis who were mostly Catholic and anti-British. There was also in this latter group a small English and Scottish presence from the period 1812–1821 when the North West Company was under Anglophone management.

The Plains Métis throughout the 19th century interacted with both the Hudson's Bay and North West companies. They ranged from Prairie du Chien, WI; Pembina, ND; St. Boniface, Manitoba; Batoche, Saskatchewan; and Edmonton, Alberta. The extended family of blood relatives was an important feature of Métis society, which was essentially patriarchal, cooperative, and migratory. They were part of the agreements with the U.S. with the Red Lake and Pembina Ojibwa, but their right of admission to the Turtle Mountain Reservation remained unresolved. After the transfer of Rupert's Land to Canada without Métis consultation, they occupied Fort Garry in Manitoba and formed a provisional government in opposition in 1869–1870. Despite negotiated terms for their rights, by 1879 they were a minority in the Manitoba legislature and many were compelled to relocate farther north and in Saskatchewan. The Canadian government refused to confirm Métis' claims along the Qu'Appelle and South Saskatchewan rivers, which led to unrest and armed resistance at Duck Lake, Fish Creek, and Batouche in 1885. Their military defeat forced some to seek refuge in Montana and North Dakota especially after the execution of Louis Riel, their political leader. Some Métis, whose lifestyles were closer to their Indian relatives, were included in Treaties Nos. 3, 4, and 6 in the Canadian Prairie provinces, whereas others continued to live on Indian reserves without legal status. In the 1980s they finally gained Canadian recognition as a separate ethnic people.

Notable Plains Métis communities are at Walhalla, Pembina, and Turtle Mountain, in North Dakota and at Wolf Point, Havre, and near Great Falls in Montana; several places in the vicinity of Winnipeg; St. Victor, Willow Bunch, and around Batouche, in Saskatchewan; Lac la Biche, St. Albert and St. Paul in Alberta. In 1991 there were estimated to be 100,000 Métis in Manitoba, 80,000 in Saskatchewan, and 60,000 in Alberta, with perhaps 30,000 in Montana and North Dakota.

Métis artwork can be found on a variety of personal clothing and trade items. Catholic teaching institutions integrated refinements to native decoration including quillwork, silk embroidery, and beadwork for coats, horse gear, and costume. They are particularly associated with the spread of floral designs among themselves and the western tribes. Rudolph Kurz in his c. 1848 journal reported "Metisse" (Métis) dressed in bright colors, semi-European, semi-Indian, with tobacco pouches, knife cases, saddles, shoes, and whips decorated with beads, porcupine quills, bird quills etc., in artistic work done by their wives and sweethearts. The Plains Métis were renowned buffalo hunters and often employed the tipi as a temporary dwelling while hunting. They also developed the so-called Red River cart for transportation. They spoke several dialects of a French-native patois called Mitchif.

Left: Dress of the Northern Ojibwa/Saulteaux/Métis men, c. 1800–1830. The man on the left wears a moose-hide open-front coat with woven and wrapped quilled epaulets at the shoulder and narrow floral and disk quillwork on the front and cuffs. He wears a hood with ears (perhaps some type of symbolic hunting aid?) and holds a braided woolen sash in chevron patterns. His moccasins have U-shaped instep vamps. The man on the right wears a woven quilled pouch around his neck with letters, a quilled knife case, front seam leggings with fur garters. He also wears a cloth hood with ribbonwork and buckskin moccasins with the center seam covered with quillwork and woven wool sash. *By permission of the artist, Dave Sager.*

Below: Francois Lucie, Métis, painted by Paul Kane (1810–1871), in 1846 at Fort Edmonton. Adding a shoulder strap to a black skin or cloth pouch in three decorative areas could have been the origin of the popular bandolier bag.

Chapter 3: Culture

WARFARE AND WEAPONS

The Ojibwa's principal areas of conflict during the historic period were their periods of warfare with the Iroquois during the 17th century, their colonial wars against the British and Americans until the War of 1812, and in the west constant conflict with the Dakota (Sioux). Despite the U.S. government's attempts to settle the differences between the Dakota and Ojibwa by agreeing a treaty boundary across Minnesota at the Prairie du Chien Treaty of 1825, attacks and retribution by both sides continued until the early reservation days of the mid-19th century.

The Ojibwa Indians of the Northeastern Woodlands had long used human scalps taken in battle as proof of a warrior's brave deeds. Their societies depended upon a man's status as a hero which required necessary evidence. The scalplock taken from an enemy's crown displayed on his war club or on his wigwam provided visible evidence of his valor. The scalp was also a token of his enemy's spiritual power; the hair at the top of the head, braided and decorated, represented and captured his soul. To lose one's hair, even if remaining alive, was to lose similar control over one's own identity. A scalp was also considered a substitute for a prisoner, who were often taken in warfare and integrated to replace fallen warriors. Replacements for dead tribal members was often an inducement to go on the warpath. Captured whites and white-intermarried traders inherited these values from their native compatriots. However, frontier warfare secularized the collection of scalps to one merely of financial worth. Northern Ojibwa hunters were generally unaffected by these conflicts which were concentrated south of their homeland.

Warfare altered radically after the arrival of the French and British who brought European weapons and trade goods. The fur trade intensified intertribal conflicts with the Iroquois forcing an Ojibwa retreat to the western Great Lakes. Later they regained large areas of the northern shore of Lake Huron. Ojibwa warriors fought alongside other Algonkians and Kahnawake Mohawks against the British during the French and Indian Wars, and joined their Ottawa and Potawatomi brothers during the

Old Northwest Rebellion of 1763. They then assisted the British in the Revolution and War of 1812. However, their active warriors were sometimes few in number, often part of coalitions of warriors of various tribes.

Conflicts for control of hunting grounds and wild rice areas were the main causes of intertribal warfare with the Dakota south and west of Lake Superior. The war between the Ojibwa and the Dakota was spread over three states and lasted 150 years. The first recorded conflict was in 1691 and earthen burial mounds still survive for each tribe's dead. The Ojibwa had already removed the Fox Indians from the mouth of the Montreal River and had settled at Madeline Island and Chequamegon Point by the late 17th century. Duluth, the French trader, tried to bring an agreement between the tribes but the massacre of a party of French traders in 1736 drew the Ojibwa into further conflict with the Dakota. The Ojibwa joined the French and Cree in northern Minnesota in fights at the Lake of the Woods and Red Lake, and alone attacked the Dakota at Fond du Lac and Mille Lacs, with intermittent conflicts along the Chippewa and Red Cedar rivers ("The Road to War") in present-day Wisconsin. As late as 1806 the Dakota tried to regain control of the wild rice beds in the Mole Lake area of Wisconsin and in the resulting battle with the Sokoagon Ojibwa over 500 were killed and buried in a common mound. The Dakota retreated westward and never attempted to reestablish themselves in this area again. The large Leech Lake band was the vanguard of the westward advancing Ojibwa; it was closest to the Dakota and hated them most. At a meeting between Chief Flatmouth of the Leech Lake band and the U.S. Agent Schoolcraft in 1832, the chief declared that the Great Spirit had decreed that hatred and war had always existed between them and never could be changed. Warfare in this area was mainly waged by small war parties sent out from their village of 200 to 300 inhabitants. The loss of life was

Below: *The Pipe Dance and the Tomahawk Dance of the Chippewa Tribe* after a painting by James Otto Lewis (1792–1858) at the Treaty of Prairie du Chien 1825. The arrangement of the feathers on the warriors' head, and the fur (skunk?) garters are probably accurate.

Above: Bowcase and quiver of buckskin and red trade cloth decorated with beadwork, and arrows with metal tips. Probably Plains Ojibwa or Métis. *Musée du Quai Branly, Paris.*

usually minimal as it had been in the east; and a retaliatory raid was considered successful if just one enemy scalp was obtained. Sometimes two or more villages formed alliances for defense or, fearing a Dakota attack, would abandon their settlements on the borderlands of the two peoples. American intervention became inevitable when white traders and then settlers moved into the tribal battle zones in present-day Wisconsin and Minnesota. The grand conference at Prairie du Chien in August 1825 between the territorial governors, William Clark and Lewis Cass, agents, military, and representatives of all the western Great Lakes tribes agreed a general peace and a dividing line between the Dakota and Ojibwa lands running southeast across Minnesota. However, peace was short-lived and full-scale warfare continued on both sides of the agreed boundary. In 1839 the Mdewkanton Dakota killed 100 Ojibwa who had visited Fort Snelling for annuities and fighting continued until late 1850s. A major battle took place on the Brule River in 1842 which was reported by the American agent Benjamin Armstrong (adopted son of Chief Buffalo) as a decisive victory for the La Pointe Ojibwa over the Dakota. His claims were later exaggerated in order to maintain the La Pointe Ojibwa's location in Wisconsin, following American plans to move them to Minnesota, as a bulwark against possible Dakota raids against settlers.

The most important indigenous weapons were bows and arrows, the ball-headed wooden club, and various types of stone clubs. By the mid-17th century iron — and later steel — hatchets and pipe-tomahawks became available from white traders together with firearms. Wooden gunstock-shaped clubs with iron or steel blades also were popular. Metal knives used for hunting and warfare were housed in buckskin sheaths decorated with porcupine quillwork and often worn around the neck. Bows were made from hickory, ash, ironwood or cedar and bowstrings of moose or deer sinew.

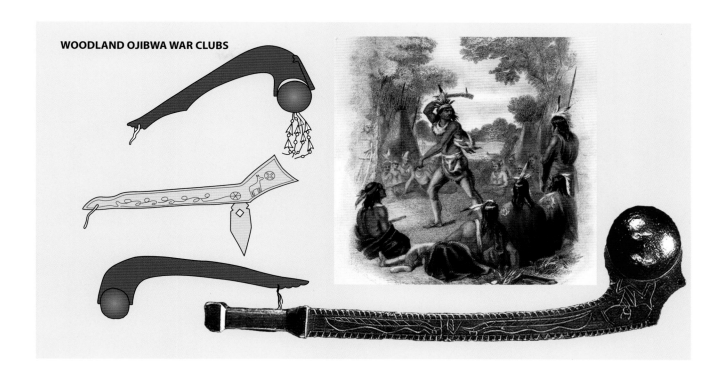

WOODLAND OJIBWA WAR CLUBS

Ball-headed war clubs were carved from the root burl or knot of extremely hard and durable wood, usually about 2.5 ft. (76 cm) long, occasionally with stone or metal spikes. They were used to mash heads and sometimes left alongside a victim pointing in the direction of his or her village. The shafts were sometimes painted or carved with pictographic inscriptions which may be readable records of the owner's identity or personal manitou, or the club's owner's war record and pictographs of the enemies he had killed. Sometimes a warrior's totemic animal was carved across the ball of the club.

By the end of the 17th century Ojibwa warriors had largely adopted firearms as their principal weapon, although the bow and wooden club were retained as a stealth weapon until the 19th century. Nevertheless major actions were usually executed with firearms and they often demonstrated a superiority of marksmanship in their use. Warriors spent their time in the acquisition of marksmanship, whereas European soldiers often relied on unaimed volley fire. However, gunpowder was a commodity only European traders could supply and so Indian hunters and warriors could quickly experience shortages in food when cut off from their supply. In the 19th century ball-headed clubs were relegated for use as ceremonial objects used mainly for display rituals.

The traditional enemies of the Plains Ojibwa were the Mandan, Hidatsa, Arikara, and Dakota; their allies were the Plains Cree and Assiniboine. Often war parties contained contingents of all three tribes engaging in mock battles before venturing towards enemy country. In spite of the ferocity of Indian warfare the numbers of actual people killed were quite small. The norm was a quick raid or ambush just before dawn and then rapid retreat before resistance could be organized.

Above Left: Typical Ojibwa clubs.

Top: Pontiac in 1763, raising the war club.

Above: Ball-headed war club, probably Ojibwa from the late 18th century. The iconography incised is perhaps the owner's personal Manitou and malevolent horned underwater serpents. A warrior's war accomplishments could also be recorded on his war club. War clubs were not just personal weapons, they were a metaphor for war. To "raise the war club" was to declare war and to "bury the war club" (or hatchet) indicated peace. *Minneapolis Institute of Art.*

Above: *An Indian Scalp Dance*, watercolor painting by Peter Rindisbacher in the 1820s in the Red River area of Southern Manitoba. Note the red and blue trade cloth leggings worn by the males and a strap dress and hood by a woman in the background. One male has a panel bag worn around his neck.

The Dakota usually retaliated against the Plains Ojibwa and Métis. Young warriors were required to paint their faces black. Returning warriors usually turned over scalps to the women and performed a scalp dance. The Plains Ojibwa possessed individual warrior bundles (collections of animal skins of significant power for the owner) but not the tribal or clan war bundles as known to their Algonkian relatives such as the Potawatomi. They used rawhide shields and stone war clubs of the Plains type. There were several men's warrior-dancing societies among the Plains Ojibwa similar to those of other Prairie and High Plains tribes, which distinguished them from Woodland Ojibwa. These included the *okitsita* (a type of tribal police) drawn from various societies such as the Big Dogs, Buffalo, Grass, and Prairie Chicken.

The grass dance or Sioux dance arrived among the Plains Ojibwa of Manitoba and Saskatchewan during the 1860s or 1870s. The distinctive men's dress of this society included the porcupine and deer-hair head roach, a crow belt, a type of back bustle with eagle feathers worn at hip level, and braids of sweetgrass worn with the belt. The ritual appears to have replaced or absorbed their own warrior societies' rituals, whereas another form, a quasi-religious ritual, spread to the Woodland Ojibwa reserves in Minnesota and Wisconsin. Secularized and modernized men's versions of these rites are the principal features at summer powwows throughout Ojibwa reserves and urban communities of recent times.

WOODLAND OJIBWA LIFESTYLE

The Ojibwa were constantly moving to obtain sufficient food. During the early historic period they were much unsettled by the incursions of the Iroquois. They usually lived in small groups and although deer, bear, and moose were the principal animals sought, in winter rabbits and beavers were important in the absence of larger game. Fish were taken in summer and winter with nets, hooks, lines, and spears. Whitefish, salmon, sturgeon, trout, and pike were taken in great quantities, particularly around the Great Lakes and south of Lake Superior. Large animals were skillfully tracked and killed with entrails removed lest the meat should putrefy. The tongue and heart were taken by a hunter to his lodge and the family women and children were directed to fetch the meat the next day. Moose were not plentiful south of Lake Superior, with deer, bear, and beaver the principal animals sought. Bears were often hunted with dogs and provided excellent meat, their oil rubbed into hair and bodies, and their fur hides used for good bedding. Feasts, songs, and prayers were addressed to Nanahbozhoo or Nanabush for the gifts of food, and failure to make offerings could lead to starvation. The bear was treated with special respect.

Berries of all kinds and wild rice were substantial parts of their diet. Berries were eaten fresh or dried for future use. Wild rice was common in most of the southern areas of Ojibwa territory. It was collected in September by means of canoes by men and women armed with long poles.

Above: "The Hunters" — Rowland W. Reed's c. 1908 photograph of Ojibwa hunters in a birchbark canoe that has the characteristic curved end silhouette of many Southwestern Ojibwa canoes.

The plant was turned into the canoe with a pole from one side while another occupant thrashed it until the grain was separated from the stem. The grain was then dried over a fire, the hull and chaff removed. Wild rice could be seasoned with maple sugar or combined with the broth of duck or deer.

An important spring activity for some Ojibwa bands was the collection of maple sap and the making of maple syrup and sugar. Single families, or sometimes several families, camped at maple sugar groves. The trees were tapped and the sap collected in birchbark buckets and stored in moose-skin vats. Women collected the sap and boiled it to make sugar and then mixed it with wild vegetables, cereal, fish, and berries ready to eat.

Ojibwas recognized the year had four seasons and 12 moons. The winter hunting season, which extended from November to March, took place after the people had split into small or family bands in the interior forests and moved to their individual family hunting grounds.

Women usually gave birth in a small temporary shade. They had no dedicated midwives, instead relying on other mothers to provide help and medicines. Babies were immediately swaddled in a small blanket and after about a month placed on a portable wooden cradleboard about 2.5 ft. long by 1.5 ft. (76 cm x 45 cm) wide and covered with cloth. A projecting bow from near the top gave protection to the infant. Secured in this manner the women carried their babies on their backs. The various feasts and ceremonies that followed a birth were intended to ensure a long and successful life. The elaborate ceremonies that followed death assured successful arrival in the afterworld. The body was kept for a day or so and dressed in the best clothes. On the feet were new moccasins painted with vermilion. The body was buried wrapped in a new blanket. At the head of the grave a small post was erected on which the clan or totem symbol of the deceased was painted or carved. The deceased was laid in an extended or flexed position and weapons, ornaments, and utensils placed in the grave, usually a small wooden structure and pole with a clan symbol erected over it.

On forest trails, warriors walked first looking for game or possible hostiles. The women came next, carrying strips of birchbark and hides for covering their wigwams. Individual families or a small group of, perhaps, three families would camp and set up their bark wigwams close together, chinked with moss and with an extra cover of cedar boughs. Children were instilled with hardihood, self-reliance, and absence of fear was cultivated. As soon as they could understand, they heard the deeds of their ancestors. Once the snow had fallen the spirits slept, so the elders and shaman could relate stories without upsetting them.

During summer months they navigated the lakes and rivers with birchbark canoes and in winter crossed the snow to track game on snowshoes made of ash and laced with thongs of moosehide. They transported heavy goods on wooden toboggans and, as already mentioned, carried their infants on wooden cradleboards strapped to their mothers' backs. Before the arrival of white European traders, they made all the essential articles they used

Above: Wild rice (*Zizania aquatica*) grows on the east coast and Northern wild rice (*Zizania palustris*) grows in shallow water in small lakes and slow-flowing streams in the Great Lakes region. Both were harvested by Indians canoeing into the plants and using "knockers" — long sticks — to bend the heads over the canoes so the grains could be threshed.

Opposite: The maple sugar industry was an important spring activity. The main photograph shows a woman tapping maple sap. **Inset:** Boiling up the syrup in front of the peaked wigwam with birchbark containers for catching sap and boiling sap.

themselves. It is probable that pre-contact Ojibwa had an equalitarian political system founded on kinship relationships acting as semi-autonomous units but linked by ties of clan membership to other, sometimes quite distant, bands and relations through marriage. There were few political leaders until the challenges of white contact and there was a tribal unity of sorts, but only based on clan membership, language, and kinship. These ties cut across bands separated by huge distances helping to unify a form of nationhood.

Their kinship system and social organization based on patrilineal clans were similar to those of the Potawatomi and Ottawa. These tribes kept together in one category relatives of a single generation. For instance, a father and his brothers and the husbands of a mother's sisters were called father or stepfather. Similarly, a mother and her sisters and the wives of father's brothers were all called mother or stepmother. Grandfathers and their brothers were called grandfather, and grandmothers and all her sisters were called grandmother. Other relatives were obtained by intermarriage between families belonging to different clans, even different tribes.

A clan was a group of actual or assumed blood relatives who traced their descent from a mythical single ancestor through the male line. None could marry within the same clan. A father and his children belonged to one clan and a mother to another clan. Among the Ojibwa clans were the Crane, Loon, Hawk, Goose, Gull, Pike, Sturgeon, Whitefish, Otter, Marten, Moose, Bear, Beaver, Caribou, Lynx, and Snake. Similar clans existed among the Potawatomi and Ottawa, and since these clans were distributed among all bands they gave each tribe a unity of sorts. Members of these clans considered themselves in a special relationship with the animal from which the clan was named. Clan symbols were often painted or carved on grave posts, wigwams, and birchbark records. During the periods of intermarriage with British and American traders, their offspring acquired new clan symbols, the Lion and Eagle respectively.

WOODLAND OJIBWA BELIEFS

The basic world view of the Great Lakes people was the belief that the natural world was animated by spirits called manitos. Animals, plants and all cosmic objects were thought of as persons which had power to affect the fortunes of individual humans. According to native cosmology the universe consisted of three parallel worlds. Above the earth arched a huge sky-dome dominated by thunderbirds with flashing eyes and flapping wings that brought rain to make the earth fertile. The earth was at the center of a large island floating on a great lake. Below these waters lay the underworld dominated by extremely powerful manitos who controlled plants, animals, and fish. The most powerful of these manitos were the underwater panthers — composite beings with horned heads and bodies of powerful cats and dragon-like tails. These beings could bestow both good and evil, controlling medicines and healing, but were also dangerous and destructive. The thunderbirds and underwater panthers were thought to

Above: Ojibwa/Saulteaux children, Berens River, Ontario 1933. Each is holding a pair of snowshoes. Berens River remains one of the most northerly communities of predominant Ojibwa people in Manitoba.

Opposite, Above: Mrs. Joe Socs, Ojibwa Nett Lake Reservation, MN, 1946, with the snowshoes she made. Inset, the diagram shows typical Ojibwa snowshoes 3 ft 9 in (1.14 m) by 1 ft 9 in (53 cm).

Opposite, Below: *The Snowshoe Dance at the First Snowfall.* George Catlin probably sketched this at Fort Snelling in 1835. It shows thanksgiving to the Great Spirit for the aid of snowshoes when hunting in winter.

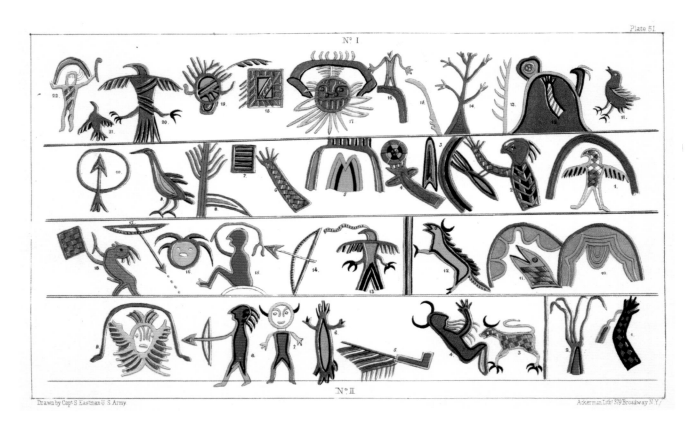

Drawn by Capt S Eastman U. S. Army.   Ackerman Lith' 379 Broadway N.Y.

Above: Painted pictographs served as mnemonic devices for recalling the spirits of the supernatural world. As here they showed a variety of conventionalized animals, birds, and thunderbirds, but also ghosts, witches, water monsters, and cosmic phenomena. Such images could be incised on birchbark scrolls, migration charts, or painted on drums, grave posts, and music boards.

be in perpetual feud. In order to survive in a world filled with dangerous supernatural powers, hunters, warriors, and women all needed to acquire the protection of a guardian spirit via a vision or dream through fasting and seclusion.

Cosmic space was further structured by the four cardinal directions at the center of which lay a path to the worlds above and below. Forest travelers and warriors on the warpath learned how to orient themselves to the power of manitos and their associated topographical features, mapping the forests with tomahawk marks on trees and red ochre paintings on rock surfaces. Various individuals had the ability to communicate with the spirit world, popularly called medicine men or shaman. They had control over supernatural power that they could control for healing or for evil purposes. They were respected and feared by the people.

Arching over these religious phenomena was a paramount deity, Kitchi-Manito (creator), although some historians now suspect the concept may be the influence of Christian missionaries. They may also have introduced ideas based upon religious orders or masonic lodges which formed the basis of the Midewiwin or Grand Medicine Society, a ceremonial complex whose rituals promoted good health, well being, and long life.

The Ojibwa superbeing was Nanahbozhoo, who gave the earth its form. In the beginning there was a great flood and with great difficulty he managed to save many of the birds and animals. To form this new world he had to obtain a small amount of earth from beneath the waters. From the raft he had constructed, Nanahbozhoo asked many birds and animals to dive to the bottom to recover some soil, but even the otter and beaver failed, all except the muskrat who finally managed to clutch some mud in each paw and in his mouth. Nanahbozhoo strewed the mud across the water until it spread and very quickly the new ground reached beyond the horizon forming a great island. He then journeyed across the great island creating the various Indian tribes and giving various customs and religions. He taught them to hunt, and to grow the sacred tobacco plant through whose smoke the Indians could communicate with the spirit world. Nanahbozhoo then withdrew north overlooking human activity. Before sleeping for winter he filled his great pipe and smoked for days, often producing the haze of an Indian summer. He was the great trickster, the agent of the creator from whom all learned that to address the Great Spirit, intermediaries and lesser spirits had to be asked. All objects had supernatural power — animals, trees, an unusual rock, waterfalls — but the most revered for their greatest power was the sun and moon. The world was full of unfriendly spirits that had to be placated. Ojibwas lived close to nature and did not envisage any great separation from the rest of creation. They had a special relationship with animals reflected in their clan names representing a large number of birds and animals. Great respect for the spirits of animals killed for food was considered a duty.

The religion of the Ojibwa was similar to that of the Potawatomi and Ottawa; however, the Ojibwa placed more emphasis on hunting charms and dreams for success in hunting. There was no special priesthood but shamans controlled the good and evil powers permeating the natural world. In early historic times the most highly organized part of the religious life of their eastern bands revolved around the Feast of the Dead — somewhat similar to that of the Huron — involving the reburial of the dead approximately every dozen years and including the reestablishing of tribal alliances. The religion of the Potawatomi and Ottawa consisted of a similar body of beliefs as well as rituals and ceremonies which included sacred bundles containing sacred objects and charms.

Above: An otter-skin medicine pouch with quillwork and metal bells. It's probably a first degree Midewiwin Society pouch.

MIDEWIWIN OR GRAND MEDICINE SOCIETY

The Midewiwin or Grand Medicine Society was the most important Ojibwa ceremonial complex. It still survives in remote areas or in secret. Its main objectives were to promote individual and community success in hunting, good health, wellbeing, and long life. Although its recent geographical center appears to have been northern Minnesota, it is said to have gained prominence around Chequamegon Bay, La Pointe, and Madeline Island in Wisconsin where a large body of Ojibwa had moved from the north shore of Lake Superior and the upper peninsula of Michigan during the early fur trade period in about the second half of the 17th century.

Rituals were usually held annually or semiannually lasting from 2 to 5 days depending on the number of initiates or candidates. Candidates selected for membership were usually male aged 12 upwards, and chosen by application, instruction, or formal invitation. There were at least four (and sometimes even up to eight) ascending degrees of membership in the society, each representing the animal spirit volunteers who had transmitted

Above: Midewiwin conductor pouches, Plains Ojibwa c. 1910–1920, usually worn around the neck. The beaded designs represent the initiate for "Mide" membership, and a water spirit. The pouches usually have small pockets corresponding to body parts containing shells which are virtually "shot" into the initiate and extracted, which represents "death" and "rebirth" into the Midewiwin Societies' varying degrees of membership.

the ritual from the creator to the receptive individuals on Earth. Pouches used for doctoring were made from the animal spirit evoked; otter skin for the first degree, then hawk, owl and bear and if applicable, eagle, wolverine, lynx, and snake (details vary). Each ascending degree of membership required fees of increasing value for the officiating priests, sponsors, and their assistants. The new member was presented with a Mide pouch representing the degree to which he had been admitted.

The ceremony took place in a large wigwam (Midewigan) where the spirit of Kitchi-Manito resided. The ritual was presided over by an instructor or sponsor and a number of priests who were all obliged to visit a sweat lodge with the candidate for purification and to appeal for a fine day and make offerings to the Great Spirit. They then entered the Midewigan circuiting the enclosure four times inside and outside. The candidate was led to the western end of the lodge where he knelt. The priest (Midas) held a medicine pouch containing the Megis (a shell), which he thrust vigorously towards the candidate's heart four times as if to shoot him. The action in effect shoots the vital spiritual power into the soul of the initiate, a baptismal act that aroused strong emotions. The priest then reapplied his medicine bags and the candidate recovered, coughing out the Megis shell that was believed to have been shot into his body. The ceremonial "death and rebirth" initiated him as a member of the society and he then distributed trade goods' gifts as a form of membership fee. During the 19th century the Midewiwin was active at Leech Lake, Fond du Lac, Mille Lac, Red Lake, and Nett Lake in Minnesota; La Pointe and Lac Courte Oreilles in Wisconsin; Berens River, Lac Seul, Rat Portage and Northwest Angle in Manitoba.

The Wabeno was a religious society whose shaman interpreted dreams, healed the sick through rituals, deriving spiritual power from fire and regarding the Morning Star as a source of power. It shared some similarities with the Midewiwin Society having both male and female members. During an induced trance-like state, members received spiritual assistance to treat patients, divining and foretelling events, and sometimes assuming animal forms. The society appears to have been described by the Jesuit fathers and was looked upon as witchcraft and jugglery. A Wabeno usually concluded with a shaking tent ceremony. It seems to have survived longest among the Saulteaux and Severn River Ojibwa-Cree of Ontario, and probably still does in remote areas.

SUN DANCE AND OTHER PLAINS OJIBWA CEREMONIES

The Sun Dance ceremony, which the Plains Ojibwa adopted from the Plains Cree, was one of the principal traits which set apart the Plains Ojibwa from their Woodland relatives. In turn the Plains Cree had obtained the rite from the Assiniboine. The ceremony was usually performed in mid-June, near the spring solstice. It was primarily directed to the thunderbirds to ask them to bring rain which encouraged the regrowth of grass and in turn the annual return of the buffalo. The ceremony was also a tribal plea to ask for good health and good fortune.

The announcement of the ceremony, usually held once a year, was made in midwinter initiated by a man in fulfillment of a vow for good health of a relative or thanks for the return of good health. At the beginning of the ritual a group of men leave the Sun Dance encampment in search of a sacred tree. These men act as warriors in their search for the tree that will form the Sun Dance lodge's center pole and a primary support in the construction of the sacred lodge. A number of forked posts about 6 ft (1.82 m) high forming an outer circle were connected together by a ring of timbers at the heads and by rafters running from the top of each post to the prepared fork at the top of the sacred center pole. The lodge was then covered with brush around the outside; an altar was arranged on the north side of the lodge consisting of a bison skull suitably decorated with ribbons, sage or sweetgrass, eagle feathers and sacred catlinite pipes. Inside the lodge special booths and screens were prepared for the dancers. Colored cloth banners were tied to the center pole and rafters as offerings to the four directions or thunders. All the ritual objects for the ceremony, which usually lasted for 4 days, were purified with prayers, sweetgrass, and incense.

Dancers had small eagle-bone whistles ornamented with ribbons or eagle "breath" feathers about their necks. They piped to the beat of the drum as they shuffled back and forth with their gaze riveted on the thunderbird's nest at the top of the center pole. The choreography of the dance was designed to call the mother bird (thunderbird) to come and feed the dancers (baby birds) who by alighting in the nest would bring rain and invigorate the prairie grass and hence

Top: "Chippewa-Cree" Sun Dance lodge at Rocky Boy Reservation, c. 1935.

Bottom: Ojibwa singers in a Wabeno lodge, Pauingassi (Fairford), Manitoba, 1933.

Above: Painted Mide figures on a drum head.

Opposite: Saulteaux trapper, c. 1910. That part of the Northern Ojibwa in the Lake Winnipeg area are usually called Saulteaux. Note his snowshoes, mittens, and skin leggings. His moccasins have the distinctive U-shaped beaded vamps over the instep. He holds a muzzle-loader supplied by the Hudson's Bay Company, and over his shoulder is slung his powder horn and bullet pouch.

Below: Girl weaving a rabbitskin blanket; Saulteaux, Little Grand Rapids Band, Manitoba, 1935.

the return of the bison and to bring good crops. Dancing continued in this manner for 4 days without dancers taking food or water for the entire period. During the third day members of the Windigokan or Clown Cult may enter the Sun Dance lodge wearing their long-nosed masks in imitation of a race of cannibalistic ice giants prominent in Ojibwa folklore. The Windigokan cult reflects the juxtaposition of the Plains Ojibwa rituals combining the Plains clown societies with the fear of the forest-dwelling ice-giant.

The Sun Dance is probably not old among Plains Ojibwa, arriving perhaps during the early 19th century and later performed on their reserves in southern Manitoba and southeastern Saskatchewan. It was observed by the ethnologists Alanson Skinner (in the early 20th century) and James Howard (in the mid-20th century). However, the latter reports the ritual at Turtle Mountain, ND, appears to have been influenced by the Dakota version of the ceremony. Both reported the Buffalo Dance to heal the sick and bring bison in times of hunger and scarcity, a type of ritual known to many central Algonkians. Other Plains-type ceremonies included the Smoking Lodge, respecting dreamed animals; the Trade Dance, performed to secure heavy snowfall making it easier to track and obtain game; and a number of warrior dancing societies such as the Prairie-Chicken, Buffalo, Big Dogs, Grass Dance, and the Okitsita, a type of tribal police well known to many northern Plains peoples. Skinner reported the Bear Dance, Big Dogs Dance, and Horse Dance on the Cowesses Reserve, Saskatchewan. However, many of the other rituals such as the Prairie-Chicken, Tea, and Grass Dance had become social dances by the 20th century.

The Plains Ojibwa man's Grass Dance is a variant of the widespread Omaha or War Dance of the Plains Indians, and probably came to the Plains Ojibwa separately from the form that spread eastward to the Woodland Ojibwa as the Drum Religion or Dream Dance. The older version of the ceremony was formerly the property of a warrior-dancing society and dedicated to the thunderbirds. The distinctive badges of the society were the roach headdress (usually deer and porcupine hair) and a feather bustle or "Crow Belt" made from the feathers of birds of prey who scavenged a battlefield, and worn at the level of the hips on the dancer's back. Braids of sweetgrass were also worn in the belt, hence the term Grass Dance. This old form of the dance had officers, drum keepers, warriors, and singers, both male and female. Dancers assumed the posture of warriors searching for and fighting their enemies when dancing. By the mid-20th century the old Grass Dance had been replaced by a more secularized version and in its modern form is a principal feature of male dances at summer powwows on all reserves and reservations. Spectators and specialist singing groups travel hundreds of miles to participate. Dancer's costume has also much changed from the old warrior type to more baroque styles with various categories offering cash prizes (see p. 125).

The old Woodland Ojibwa Dream Dance was never widely adopted by their Plains relatives although the Peyote religion, a combination of Indian and Christian practices that developed in Oklahoma, has made its way to the Canadian Reserves.

Chapter 4:
Material Culture

INDIGENOUS MATERIALS AND CLOTHING

Before the advent of European trade goods, native clothing consisted of tanned hides of deer, elk, moose, and other animals. Sewing threads were made of nettle-weed fiber or sinew of deer or moose that could be split into very fine strands. In tanning deer hide, the flesh side of a green hide was cleaned off with the chiseled end of a deer or moose shinbone tool (or sharp metal knife) and then soaked in clear water for 2 or 3 days, after which hair was first cut off then scraped off with a bone or horn tool or, later, an iron blade set in a wooden handle (dehairing). The damp hide was soaked in a mixture of animal brains and water until they were almost completely absorbed. Remaining hair, flesh, or liquid that still adhered was scrapped off. The now-shrunken and thickened hide was pulled and stretched on a frame to which it was attached by leather thongs or basswood fibers. The hide was worked and softened by an implement, formerly a rock or an elk horn, later an iron tool bent at right angles to the handle, until pliable and dry. Some hides were smoked over a fire of cedar bark (or other woods) until a characteristic light brown color that gave the hide better rain-resistant qualities. The Ojibwa have a repu-tation for producing excellent tanned skins. In Ontario and northern Minnesota the Ojibwa formerly wove rabbit skin blankets for use in extremely cold weather (see opposite).

Aboriginal ceremonial skin clothing was probably prin-cipally decorated with paint obtained from natural plant and bark dyes applied as a liquid or powder, sometimes impressed with a bone tool or stamp. Porcupine and bird quills were flattened and dyed, and loom-woven into bands with geometric patterns. Other quillwork techniques included wrapping bark slats, checkerweave, and several

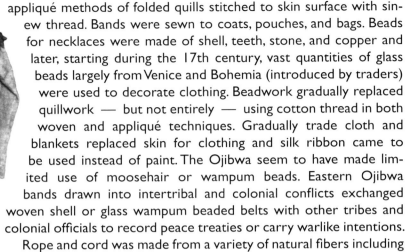

appliqué methods of folded quills stitched to skin surface with sinew thread. Bands were sewn to coats, pouches, and bags. Beads for necklaces were made of shell, teeth, stone, and copper and later, starting during the 17th century, vast quantities of glass beads largely from Venice and Bohemia (introduced by traders) were used to decorate clothing. Beadwork gradually replaced quillwork — but not entirely — using cotton thread in both woven and appliqué techniques. Gradually trade cloth and blankets replaced skin for clothing and silk ribbon came to be used instead of paint. The Ojibwa seem to have made limited use of moosehair or wampum beads. Eastern Ojibwa bands drawn into intertribal and colonial conflicts exchanged woven shell or glass wampum beaded belts with other tribes and colonial officials to record peace treaties or carry warlike intentions.

Rope and cord was made from a variety of natural fibers including basswood, various barks, nettle fiber, and Indian hemp. Wood carving by men included bowls, spoons, weapons, and some ceremonial paraphernalia such as spirit dolls. Womens' tasks included all weaving, quill and bead embroidery, preparing skins and making birchbark objects. Household containers such as twined bags were made from basswood bark fiber, nettle fiber, Indian hemp, bison wool, then later yarn and commercial wool. The Ojibwa made checked-weave cedar bark bags to hold wild rice. Woven split-wood baskets that appear to have been adopted from eastern tribes and perhaps European-inspired, supplanted the more traditional type of basket.

There are no credible images of Ojibwa Indians until the late 17th century when males were shown tattooed and wearing only breechclouts and moccasins. A few mens' skin shirts have survived from the 18th century in museum collections with tube-like fitted torsos and sleeves. Most important to both sexes were hide robes and furs for winter use and a number of important examples have survived from the 18th century enigmatically painted with mixtures of realistic and geometric designs, however none have been documented specifically Ojibwa. Mens' leggings of buckskin (and later of trade cloth) were separate tubes hitched to a waist belt. The Northern Ojibwa wore open-fronted moose-skin coats. The warrior's porcupine and deer-hair head roach originated among the Woodland tribes to augment the scalplock, and ceremonial headdresses of the western bands displayed buffalo horns. Men wore fur turbans and spectacular necklaces of grizzly bear claws were worn ceremonially. Early women's clothing consisted of a knee or calf-length wraparound deerskin skirt with the edges meeting on the left side, a style that survived with the later trade-cloth skirts. The western bands favored a dress made from two deer skins, one forming the front, the other the back. Another old-style dress, originally of skin but later of trade cloth, had a skirt that came up to the armpits and held in place by straps over the shoulders (the "strap dress"). Sometimes separate sleeves were added (in cold weather) and a sash went around the waist.

continued on p. 72

SKIN COATS

Skin coats from the Subarctic Swampy Cree and Northern Ojibwa of the 18th century were constructed with sides and back of one piece of moosehide with sleeves sewn in at right angles. East Cree and Nascapi coats were more tailored, sometimes with added gussets at the back. Cree/Ojibwa painted design elements were originally ordered along a rectilinear grid in contrast to the paintings on Nascapi coats which followed the curving lines of the seams and the tapering of gussets. The Cree/Ojibwa added quilled bands at the shoulders, and occasionally quilled chest disks. Nascapi coats are invariably of caribou hide, whereas the Cree/Ojibwa coats that survive are predominantly of moosehide. It is probable the original garment for both men and women was a tunic-type pulled over the head, although a moose skin is large enough to wrap around a man's body. However, the main features of the man's coat were influenced by successive European fashions and military uniforms from the 17th century onwards. These included added collars, and epaulets of woven porcupine quillwork at the shoulders in woven geometric designs. Later, during the first half of the 19th century, the Red River Métis, descendants of Cree and Ojibwa, made highly tailored skin coats and decorated them with narrow porcupine-quilled floral designs. Some authorities believe that all open-fronted coats are based upon European garments, and the addition of shoulder epaulets on Ojibwa coats derive from military ornamentation and hence are sometimes called "Captain's coats." Kurz (1970) notes the "Saulteurs" (Ojibwa) and other northern Plains tribes were using trade blankets and making coats from them similar to the blanket coats of the Americans about 1850. These coats had hoods and from the peak one sees a feather for decoration.

Left: Late 18th century moosehide coat, Northern Ojibwa or Cree type. Painted, with geometric and circular elements, and with quilled strips and shoulder epaulets.

Opposite, Above: Moose-skin coat (back) probably Northern Ojibwa or Swampy Cree, Ontario, c. 1780. Linear and circular painting and quillwork in red, yellow, black, white, and ochre. Long, straight-sided collarless coat with center front opening; the body formed from a single piece of hide with sleeves added. Fringe ends are ochre-dyed thongs with red-dyed hair tassels or the bottom edge cut and quill-wrapped. Speyer Collection, Canadian Museum of History, Gatineau, Quebec.

Opposite, Below: Moosehide coat, Métis, mid-19th century. The later form of coat, fitted, with refined collar and cuffs. Métis women were skilled porcupine quillers, often using delicate floral patterns. Many Métis settled along the Red River after the merging of the Hudson's Bay and North West companies resulted in redundancies. Many were of Ojibwa and Ottawa ancestry.

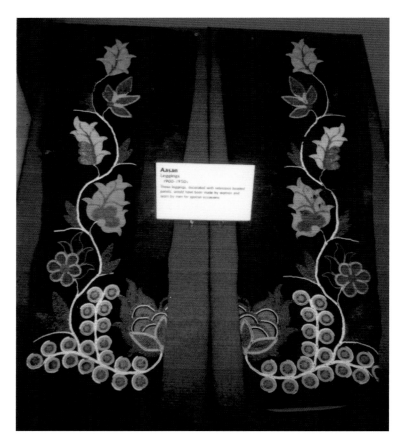

LEGGINGS

Men's buckskin leggings extended from the ankle almost to the hip and were held in place by a thong tied to a belt. They were not as wide as women's leggings. After the introduction of commercially woven cloth — usually broadcloth, strouds, or later velveteen — leggings were folded tubes with the seam on the outside, tied to a belt and also held below the knee by quilled or beaded garters.

Left: Chief Tanaghte, or Wabumagoging (Eclipse), of the Batchewana Ojibwa band, from near Sault Ste. Marie. He holds a fan and pipe, wears a coat probably made of skin, belt, arm bands, headdress with eagle feathers, cloth leggings, and buckskin moccasins. He was a delegate to Lord Elgin in Montreal c. 1849. From a painting by Cornelius Krieghoff (1815–1872).

Opposite, Above: Two pairs of Ojibwa men's leggings. Black velveteen (a cotton fabric resembling velvet) and cloth with floral beadwork, c. 1910. Lac du Flambeau, WI and Leech Lake, MN.

Opposite, Below Left: David Shoppenagon (?–1911), a Michigan Ojibwa originally from the Saginaw River. Later moved to the upper part of the Lower Peninsula. He was an expert trapper and guide. His grandfather signed the Treaty of Greenville in 1795. He is pictured here wearing trade cloth leggings and with his wife and daughter.

Opposite, Below Right: A pair of mid-19th century Ojibwa or Ottawa (Odawa) men's leggings, the back and front of trade cloth, and decorated with beadwork and ribbonwork. They are similar to the pair worn by David Shoppenagon.

MOCCASINS

Ojibwa moccasins varied considerably in different locations and different periods, and run through most of the true moccasin construction forms. Most of the early examples are **Type A** — the one-piece moccasin with front and heel seams, and ankle collars turned down, sometimes decorated with quillwork. Two rare **Type B** examples from the 18th century have been attributed to the Ojibwa. These have a modest tongue and V-shaped gore. However, the most common is **Type C**, particularly during the 19th century. These have a straight toe seam and inverted T-shaped heel seam, usually with collars turned down, with a characteristic U-shaped vamp or apron (sometimes multilayered with skin and cloth), often partially decorated with beadwork. Many Southern Ojibwa (U.S. Chippewa) moccasins are of this type, on the other hand the Northern Ojibwa, or Saulteaux of Canada, often have solidly beaded vamp and collars. The eastern Ojibwa, the Mississauga, sometimes used **Type D** with no toe seam and a large vamp with a heavily puckered seam to the bottom unit. Howard (1964) gives five construction types for the Plains Ojibwa, Types A, C, and D as above; also **Type F**, the Plains shoe, and **Type E**, the side-seam form. Occasionally narrow gores were added to the toe and heel seams on true moccasin forms. Moccasins made by mixed Ojibwa and Cree, and Métis varied little from those of their parent tribes.

Above: Type F moccasins, probably Plains Ojibwa, with a separate soft sole and solid beaded front. From the Lower Torchwood Hills area.

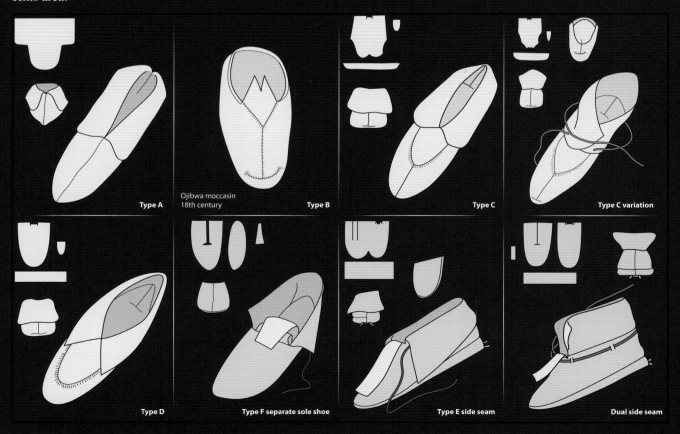

Type A

Ojibwa moccasin
18th century   Type B

Type C

Type C variation

Type D

Type F separate sole shoe

Type E side seam

Dual side seam

Top and Above Right: Cree or
Plains Ojibwa moccasins, c. 1910, of
moosehide with fully beaded fronts in
geometric designs. The seams
between the top and bottom units
slope up to the heel, the rare dual side
seam construction.

Above: Ojibwa (probably Northern
Ojibwa-Cree) Type C moccasin with
inverted T-shaped heel seam and
straight toe seam, c. 1890. They are
made of smoked moosehide, with a
cloth vamp with horsehair-wrapped
piping, cloth collar with woven beadwork in thunderbird designs. Heavy
burlap or similar ankle wrap.

Right: Ojibwa Type C moccasins,
c. 1900, with a center toe seam coming
almost to a point, inverted T-shaped
heel seam, U-shaped cloth vamp or
aprons and turned-down collars.

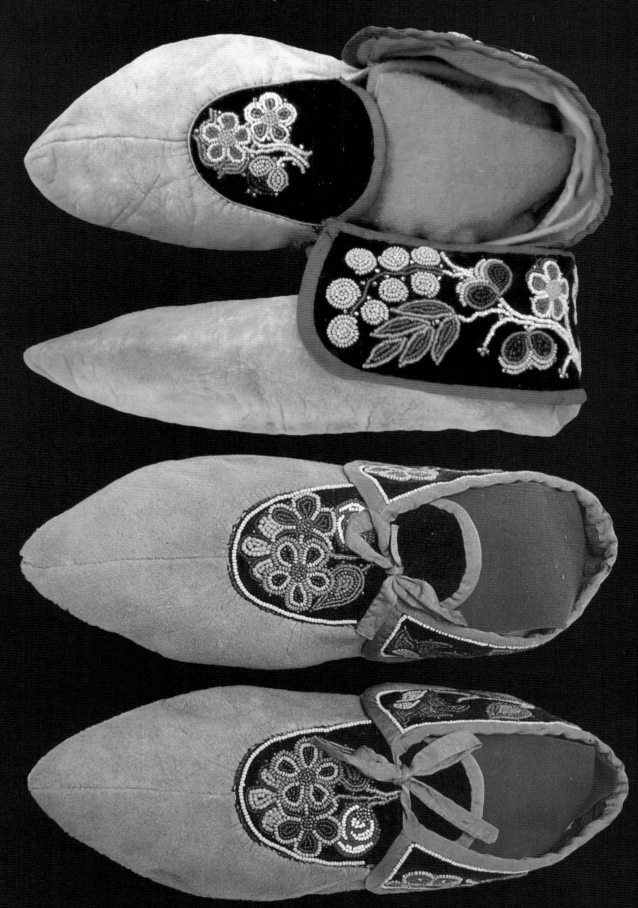

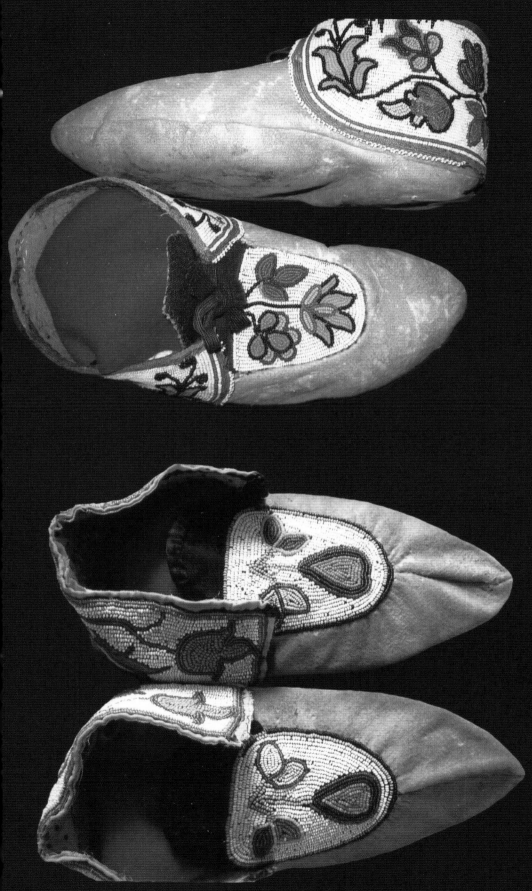

Left: Saulteaux (marginal Plains Ojibwa) moccasins, c. 1900. They were constructed from unsmoked buckskin, with a side seam running around the outside and an inverted T-shaped heel seam. This indicates a rare hybrid form of moccasin from the late 19th century from the marginal Plains and Parklands people of Canada who were of Ojibwa (Saulteaux) and Cree origin. The vamp-tongue and cuff are constructed with a type of "seed bag" material and they are decorated with floral beadwork with a white background.

Below Left: Probably Northern Ojibwa moccasins, c. 1910. Moosehide with burlap and cloth vamps and fully beaded collars.

Opposite, Above: Chippewa (Southern Ojibwa) moccasins, c. 1900. Buckskin with velveteen collars and vamps with thread-sewn beadwork. Classic Type C with inverted T-shaped heel seam and straight toe seam.

Opposite, Below: Buckskin moccasins with center seam, T-shaped heel seam, velvet vamp, and collars. The vamp and collars are decorated with floral beadwork.

Opposite, Above Left: A birch-bark and reed wigwam with bark receptacles and cradleboard, at the Waswagoning Indian village, Lac du Flambeau Reservation, WI.

Opposite, Above Right: Conical-shaped wigwam used by a family in the maple sugar camp.

Opposite, Below: Early 20th century bark house at Ponemah Point, MN, an Ojibwa community on the Red Lake Reservation. It has a roof of Norway pine bark, with side walls of elm bark.

Below: The dome-shaped wigwam of the Woodland Indian tribes — Ojibwa, Menomini, Potawatomi, etc. A wigwam was constructed by driving saplings, usually peeled iron wood, securely into the ground in either an ellipse or circle. Opposite poles were brought together in arches, overlapped and tied with grass basswood fiber. In some instances the sides were covered with bulrush mats and the top with birchbark; in others the framework was entirely covered with bark — either birch, ash or elm. The roof and sides were held in position by overlapping cords of basswood weighted by logs or stones, or sometimes by poles which were leaned against the sides. The type sketched is typical of the Great Lakes native people.

Both men and women wore buckskin moccasins of the basic type known throughout eastern North America. A one-piece buckskin moccasin with a front seam over the instep to the toe and a heel seam with an inverted T-shape at the back. However, from the late 18th century until today moccasins consisted of three pieces — the bottom-top, a U-shaped vamp or tongue, and an ankle collar — and were decorated with beadwork. A number of other forms have been used including separate-sole and side-seam moccasins by the Plains Ojibwa.

Men wore finger-woven garters and sashes originally constructed from native-made fibers, and later of wool and yarn in diamond and zigzag designs, and bags of twined vegetable fiber or yarn were used by both men and women. Men wore finger-woven sashes as turbans, also otter-fur turbans and numerous arrangements for feathers attached to the hair and braided scalplocks, usually worn erect by warriors during times of war or horizontally in times of peace.

Tobacco was grown and used as a ritual incense when smoked establishing a bond between individuals, travelers, and traders. Pipe bowls were made of red catlinite, slate, or sandstone and sometimes carved with spirit, human, or animal figures. Bowls were fitted with long wooden stems often carved and quilled. These stems decorated with feathers such as those of the woodpecker (associated with thunderbirds), or painted, could be used without the bowl as wands in invocational rituals. Such wands are referred to as calumets, a term of French origin. Bowl and stem together were smoked to seal friendship or treaties, hence peace pipes. Calumets were often used in connection rituals between Indians and French clergy during conversion ceremonials in the 17th and 18th centuries.

USE OF BIRCHBARK

The white birch, which grows throughout the northeastern United States and adjacent Canada, was used extensively by the Woodland tribes of the Great Lakes. The bark, peeled in early summer, was used for canoes and wigwams. It can be torn crosswise (similar to cloth) but is waterproof, tough, and durable against decay. Birchbark was used for utensils such as maple-sap buckets; when heated formed into dishes; and memory-aiding "rolls" with religious pictographic symbols recording tribal lore for Midewiwin Society members, and migration charts. Mats for covering wigwams were made from strips of bark overlapped and sewn together with basswood fiber. Ends were strengthened by attaching strips of cedar horizontally. These mats could be removed from the framework of a wigwam and carried to a new camp site. Although the term "wigwam" has been given to a number of different shaped dwellings, it is commonly applied to the dome-shaped structure consisting of poles planted in the ground and brought together in arches and covered with bark or sometimes bulrush (cattail) mats. For additional warmth in winter, a second row of mats could be placed around the entire lodge

Doorway

Above: A large dome-shaped birchbark Ojibwa wigwam, c. 1900.

Right: Dome-shaped Ojibwa wigwam with coverings of birch-bark on the roof and bulrush mats for the walls. Coverings were held in position with cords of basswood fiber, the ends weighted with stones or pieces of wood. Platforms for sleeping, and rush mats are shown inside. Mille Lacs Indian Museum, Onamia, MN.

Above: Diorama at the Mille Lacs Indian Museum, Onamia, MN, of the interior of an Ojibwa bark and reed lodge showing domestic activities during winter. A woven cattail reed mat and woven yarn bag are shown in the foreground.

Left: The Ojibwa peaked lodge or tipi-shaped wigwam as it might appear in winter, as seen in the Mille Lacs Indian Museum, Onamia, MN. The poles would usually be covered with birchbark (but sometimes other bark). Rush mats and birchbark receptacles shown inside. Note the snowshoes and firewood.

Above: Lucy Clark, Ojibwa, holding a birchbark basket used for collecting maple syrup, 1925.

Opposite, Above: Hunter in birchbark canoe calls a moose with a "birchbark call" to lure big game. Roland W. Reed photograph, 1908.

Opposite, Below: Details of a 2 ft. 8 in. (85 cm) long model of an eastern Ojibwa canoe, c. 1900.

overlapping the first. These mats were held in place by strips of basswood. Besides the round or oval-shaped wigwams, peaked lodges, dwellings resembling a broad low house and tipi-shaped lodges, all covered with birchbark or reeds were also common. The Plains Indian tipi was also adopted by the Plains Ojibwa of Manitoba and beyond. The Ojibwa of the White Earth Reservation have also employed the Plains type tipi in recent times.

Birchbark household receptacles included baskets, boxes, water pails, boiling vessels, and trays for wild rice. These articles were cleverly fashioned by different cuts and folds and sewn with spruce and other split roots. Some utensils were decorated with border and curvilinear (later floral patterns) designs by scraping away the darker surface layer of the inner bark that became the outside of the receptacle. In early spring maple sap was boiled down in birchbark vessels and made into sugar. Also wild rice, cured meat, and sugar could be safely stored in birchbark containers or in underground containers.

The function of engraved birchbark scrolls of the sacred Midewiwin Society was to preserve its origin traditions, migrations, and instructions. However, mide-pictographs also appeared on hide drums, or carved in the sides of drums, or painted and engraved on wooden panels and grave boards. Midewiwin birchbark scrolls are pictorial narratives on which are recorded memory aids for the singing of songs and recitation of oral traditions during ritual procedures. Both smaller song scrolls and the larger Midewiwin scrolls exhibit images and signs that are arranged to tell a story.

A wide variety of containers were made from birchbark. Simple maple-sap containers were heated and bent into shape, dish-shaped for wild rice trays, and truncated pyramid-shaped containers with rounded corners. The seams and folds were laced with basswood fiber with holes caulked with balsam gum or pitch made from spruce gum.

Sometime, probably during the 18th century, the art of decorating non-functional items of barkwork with dyed porcupine quills seems to have spread from the Micmac of Nova Scotia and the adjacent areas of Canada to the Ojibwa-Ottawa groups, particularly those centering around Manitoulin Island, Ontario and Arbre Croche, MI. In recent times the craft appears as far west as Saskatchewan. The porcupine quills collected in spring are soaked in water until soft, dyed, then the sharp ends of unflattened quills are pushed through holes in the bark made with an awl and their ends trimmed off. All manner of decorated bark work was produced — boxes, dishes, purses, model canoes, and fan handles — with mainly floral designs, but increasingly in recent times with realistic designs of animals and birds. There was limited use of moosehair embroidery on bark among the Ojibwa or Ottawa, although bark cut-outs sewn to birchbark objects were known among the Canadian Ojibwa. Native dyes were replaced by commercial dyes during the 19th century.

Birchbark is ready to be collected when the first strawberry is ripe and the bark peels easily from the trees leaving no permanent damage. Sweetgrass, collected in early summer, is sometimes sewn around the edges of bark containers with black cotton thread that helps to strengthen the rims and corners. Sweetgrass has a pleasant fragrance and, once braided, is an important religious material item.

BIRCHBARK CANOES

Canoes, snowshoes, and toboggans were the invention of the native people of North America. All these were adopted by European colonists, but the canoe most impressed the new arrivals. The earliest European explorers of the North Atlantic coast took a number back to England, so taken were they by this means of transportation.

The distribution of the birchbark canoe followed that of white or paper birch (*Betula papyrifera*). This included much of Canada and the northeastern United States in various areas of cool, moist climate. In this land of lakes and rivers the canoe was a most important item in Ojibwa life and culture, and the only means of travel and transportation over huge distances. It was a craft adopted by whites as the most expedient means of transporting furs and goods. The white man made changes to its size to become freight-bearing vessels of relatively huge proportions, often 40 ft. (12 m) long and 5 ft. (1.5 m) wide (the Montreal canoe). The ordinary Indian family canoes were usually under 18 ft. (5.5 m) in length.

The fur trade brought the white man's ax, saw, knife, and awl, which greatly facilitated the speed that canoes could be made; usually about 14 days by an expert canoe maker with the help of his family and friends, including time to collect materials. For

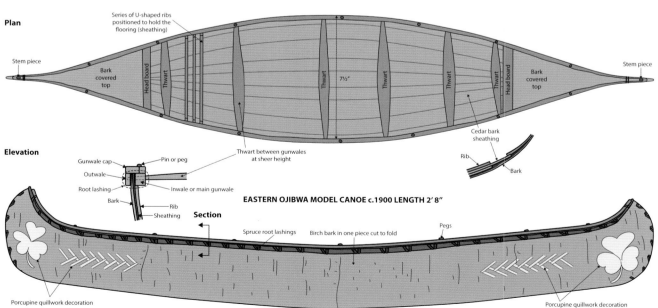

Plan

Series of U-shaped ribs positioned to hold the flooring (sheathing)

Stem piece

Bark covered top

Head board

Thwart

Thwart

7½°

Thwart

Thwart

Thwart

Head board

Bark covered top

Stem piece

Cedar bark sheathing

Rib

Bark

Elevation

Gunwale cap

Pin or peg

Outwale

Inwale or main gunwale

Root lashing

Bark

Rib

Sheathing

Section

Thwart between gunwales at sheer height

EASTERN OJIBWA MODEL CANOE c.1900 LENGTH 2′ 8″

Spruce root lashings

Birch bark in one piece cut to fold

Pegs

Porcupine quillwork decoration

Porcupine quillwork decoration

lashing the crossbars (thwarts), gunwales, seams and such the roots of spruce, jack pine or tamarack was collected and split. A selected birch tree was chosen and felled. An incision along the length of the bark was carefully made and sheets of bark peeled away. White cedar was used for the floor planks, sheathing, ribs, prows, and gunwales. The prow pieces, laminated and curved, gave the canoe its distinctive end profiles.

Construction began on a dished ground surface over which the length of the bark was positioned. A building frame composed of gunwale members and temporary thwarts was placed over it with large stones to hold it in position. Later the building frame was raised to the gunwale height. The basic form was held between guide-post stakes on either side and temporary thwarts. Slits in the bark were made to shape the canoe, usually sewn by women with spruce root and later caulked with pine resin. The gunwales were raised to the sheer height and thwarts inserted, floor planks added and held in position by a series of ribs pounded into position throughout the canoe length. Next, the prow pieces or laminated stem pieces were introduced. These gave the canoe its characteristic end silhouettes — often they are a clue to tribal origin — and sometimes a so-called man-board protected the stern carved with totemic symbols.

The Eastern Ojibwa canoe profile usually had a very short hard curve at the stem head, a large curve at the forefoot, and a straight section between. One major Western Ojibwa canoe profile was characterized by a full rounded curve between the stem head and the forefoot, producing a profile considered to be the most graceful of all canoes.

Canoes of average size were usually propelled by two people with paddles carved out of cedar (by means of a crooked knife) about 4 to 5 ft. (1 to 1.5 m) long with a blade about 5 in. (12 cm) wide. For portaging from lake to lake (or river) the paddles were tied to boards across the gunwales, the canoe carried overhead with the weight born on the shoulders.

Birchbark canoes were still being made and used particularly for hunting, fishing, and for the collection of wild rice until the early 20th century when they were largely replaced by commercial and powered craft. However, there has been some revival and examples made for museums. During the fur-trading days the Ottawas' freighting canoes sometimes used canvas sails embellished with painted designs of mythical creatures and prows decorated with porcupine quillwork.

Above: Ojibwa couple carrying a canoe to go fishing. Many canoe construction details are shown: pine resin caulked bark seams, gunwales, thwarts, ribs, and sheathing.

Opposite:
1 Ojibwa Indians making a canoe on prepared dished ground. Bark held with stones and guide post. Long Lake, Ontario. *Library and Archives Canada, PA-043591*

2 Birchbark canoe, bark torch (for night fishing) and fish spear. Waswagoning Indian Village, Lac du Flambeau, WI.

3 Details of canoe construction at the prow. It shows the guide post stakes on either side; a floor plank ready to be positioned; the laminated stem piece (used to profile the end curve); and the gunwales raised to the sheer-height. Display at the Peterborough Canoe Museum, Ontario.

4 Canoe construction showing the gunwales lashed together, thwarts, and ribs before trimming. The stem piece is held between two posts. Mille Lacs Reservation, 1959.

5 A finished canoe by Wayne Valliere, a project with the University of Wisconsin, Madison, Faculty of Art and Folklore.

Below: Birchbark model canoe with a warrior figure. The canoe is decorated with porcupine-quilled floral designs. Probably Odawa or Ojibwa. c. 1850.

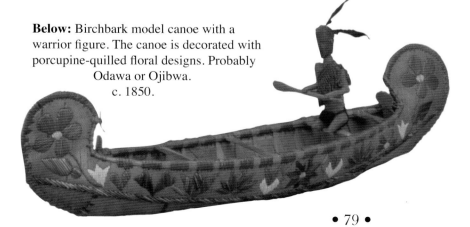

NATIVISTIC DRESS OF LATER TIMES

By the early 19th century the Eastern Ojibwa had largely adopted white man's clothing and the southeastern bands were using traded broadcloth and calico. Blankets were used as robes, red or blue cloth for men's and women's leggings and beaded buckskin moccasins. Men wore fur turbans with eagle feathers tipped with red flannel or red-dyed horsehair, evidence of war honors. Men's hair was worn long and braided, and when going on the warpath the scalplock was decorated. During this period women also wore broadcloth garments held in place by straps over the shoulders, a style superseded by the late 19th century by the Euro-American form of dresses made from black velveteen with border decorations of silk ribbon and full skirts decorated with floral beadwork.

About 1850, the wearing of large cloth bandolier bags over the shoulders came into vogue, and these gradually became a sort of national badge, an ethnic symbol forever associated with the 19th century Ojibwa, and proudly worn at ceremonies by men and sometimes women. Woven beaded bags and accessories in geometric designs were produced into the 1880s, then realistic floral designs almost totally replaced the traditional geometric patterns for both men's and women's ritual attire. Men's shirts were decorated with panels of beadwork or a cape-like yoke with breechcloths and leggings all covered with floral beadwork. One interesting style of women's dress appears to have developed among the Plains Ojibwa but was soon adopted by their Woodland relatives and worn for dances: the "jingle dress." These were originally a black cotton dress decorated with ribbons and fringed with metal cones designed to contribute to the sound of the drum when the wearer moved to the rhythm of the songs. This style continues to be very popular today and has spread to many other tribal groups in the U.S. and Canada.

Some bands of Plains Ojibwa combined both Woodland and Plains elements in their ceremonial dress. Skin shirts were worn by men. After about 1850 leaders wore similar shirts of trade cloth in blue, green, and red stroud cloth with beaded strips and discs. Buckskin or cloth leggings, folded with the seam on the outside, were held at the waist and knee with yarn or beaded knee garters. Men wore skin or cloth breechcloths. Bison robes were worn by both men and women, but later replaced by trade blankets. Women wore the Plains-type dress of two complete elk or antelope hides, one front and one back, tails up and folded back to form a cape-like top. The traditional Woodland "strap dress" was also used although it had largely disappeared by 1900. It hung from the shoulders with two straps, and had detachable sleeves and a cape-like extension hanging down the back.

Later Plains Ojibwa costumes, both men's and women's, also changed. Tailored men's suits decorated with geometrical or floral beadwork with the intrusive circle bonnets have now given way to the costumes associated with the Grass Dance complex. They are largely cloth, decorated with beaded rosettes and commercial fringes, crowned with porcupine roaches and beaded shoulder harnesses. Women's costumes have taffeta or felt dresses, fringes with or without separate skirt or blouse, decorated with floral beadwork, sequinwork, or rosettes. Occasionally, older black velvet

continued on p. 85

Above: Jingle dress in the Wisconsin History Museum. The jingles were once made from chewing tobacco can lids, rolled into cones.

Opposite, Above: Ojibwa Indian mending canoe with lodges in background, c. 1913. Photographed by Carl G. Linde.

Opposite, Below and Inset: Canoes were essential to assist the collection of wild rice. The inset image shows people gathering the rice that has collected in the canoe.

PLAINS OJIBWA SHIRTS

1 Sketch drawn by Sidney Hall of the Saulteaux leader Louis O'Soup, or Back Fat, at Fort Qu'Appelle when meeting Gov. Gen. Lord Lorne on August 19, 1881. O'Soup is wearing a shirt now in the British Museum.

2 This trade cloth shirt once belonged to Standing Elk, Turtle Mountain, Plains Ojibwa.
Today it is in the Plains Indian Museum, Browning, MT The beaded arm strips have integral disks and the beadwork on red cloth around the neck and cuffs has Woodland border patterns. The shirt probably dates from the 1880s.

3 Similar example of a Plains Ojibwa trade cloth shirt with integral disks within the armband strips and Woodland-style beadwork around the neck. Made c. 1880. North Dakota Historical Society, Bismarck, ND.

4 Buckskin shirt with beaded strips in floral and geometrical designs. The hybrid forms of decoration are typical of the Plains Ojibwa. Musée du Quai Branly, Paris. Photograph Lionel Lacaze.

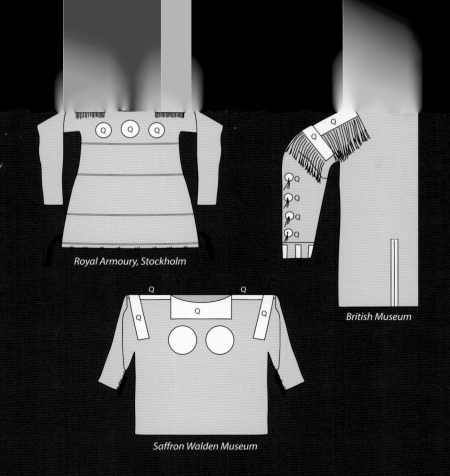

Royal Armoury, Stockholm

British Museum

Saffron Walden Museum

Glasgow Museum

Q=Porcupine quilled areas

5 Late 18th–early 19th century Ojibwa-Cree fitted male tunics of moose/caribou/cloth showing some common characteristics of Subarctic skin coats with Plains ceremonial dress of the 19th century.

6 Man wearing the trade cloth and beaded shirt now in the Plains Indian Museum, Browning, MT, once owned by Standing Elk, a Plains Ojibwa of Turtle Mountain, ND.
This man is also likely a Plains Ojibwa, c. 1900.

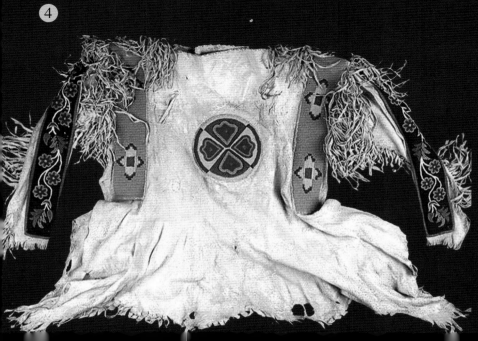

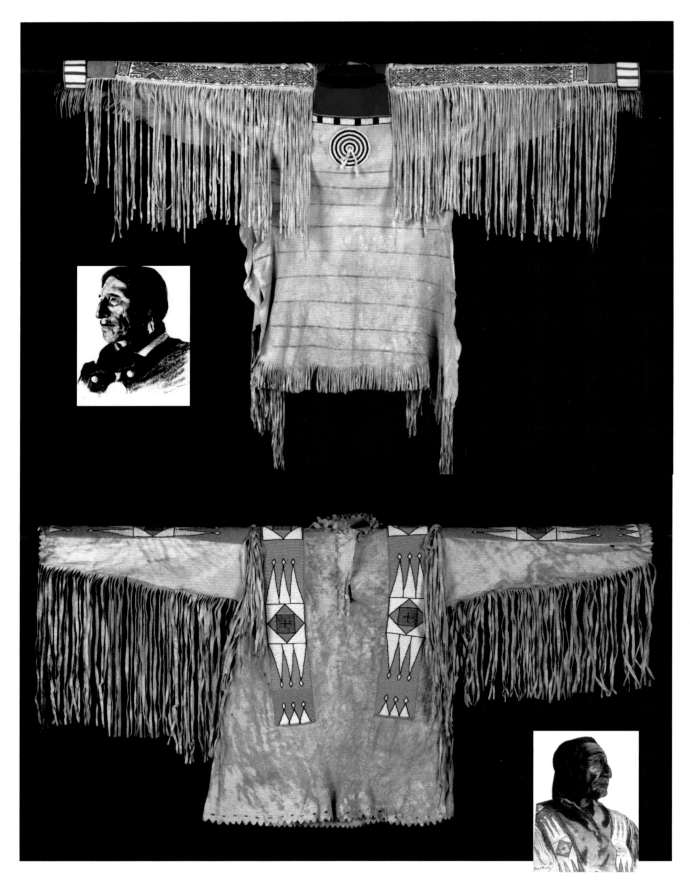

dresses are still seen. All have echoes of the past, but the materials used are mainly commercial cloth and fringes.

There was a wide variety of men's headdresses. Horned bonnets were originally common as ceremonial gear with the fur fillet as an everyday item. Crown war bonnets or circle bonnets were adopted in the 19th century. The roach may have predated the Grass Dance complex spreading from the south, but is the major headdress today for male dance attire. In very recent times ceremonial and powwow costumes have been influenced by styles from the Sioux and from Oklahoma into general Pan-Indian styles.

FLORAL DECORATION

The Métis settlements on the Red River in present-day Manitoba, and probably other locations, became a confluence of various tribal and European frontier art styles about 1800. From this mixed ethnic population various floralistic embroidery styles developed and ultimately spread across northern Canada, the Great Lakes, Northern Plains, and American Plateau by the end of the 19th century. Floral embroidery was taught to Indian girls of various tribes in Catholic mission schools in the St. Lawrence Valley during the 17th century. These designs used moosehair and porcupine quillwork, but there does not seem to be a direct link to the large realistic floral beadwork designs so popular with the Southwestern Ojibwa in the second half of the 19th century. However, an Algonkian native tradition of double-curve and simple plant-like forms in painted designs on coats and etched on birchbark work appears to be old, if not aboriginal.

Simple narrow quilled designs appear on Northern Ojibwa, Cree, and Métis artwork of the late 18th and early 19th centuries that may have been the influence of French Métis moving west with the fur trade. Another source of floral designs, such as rose and thistle motifs, is likely from the Cree's connection with the British in the James Bay area. Yet another possible influence may be the Northern European designs introduced by settlers in the American Midwest. Perhaps influenced by all these sources, complex floral compositions were created in the western Great Lakes area by the second half of the 19th century. Flowers, leaves, and fruit from different plants were freely combined. Four and five-petaled flowers are seen overlapping each other in subtle shaded color combinations connected by black-beaded veins.

However, other geometric design motifs did not disappear. These motifs are often associated with nature. An example is the "otter tail" used as a border design in beadwork; lightning designs and conventionalized thunderbird designs were also used in conjunction with floral beaded patterns. The huge range of seed bead colors available enabled women to produce works of art with as many as 30 different colors and shades on a single piece such as a bandolier bag.

Opposite, Above: Man's buckskin shirt with painted horizontal stripes and loom-woven beaded strips. Given by the Saulteaux (Plains Ojibwa) Chief Yellow Quill to Lt. Gov. Alexander Morris in June 1876 at the conclusion of treaty negotiations. The woven beadwork reflects their Woodland origins. Yellow Quill's descendants today are mostly at Swan Lake Reserve, Manitoba. The Kisistin(o) and Nut Lake reserves, Saskatchewan were once also known as Yellow Quill's reserves as a result of signing Treaty No. 4 in 1874.

Opposite, Below: Man's buckskin shirt with beaded strips given by Night Bird (Nepahpenais), Saulteaux (Plains Ojibwa) to Edmund Morris the artist (son of Alexander Morris), c. 1908. Night Bird was from the Cowesses(s) or O'Soup Reserve in the Qu'Appelle Valley, Saskatchewan. However, Night Bird is said to have obtained the shirt from a Cree who lived on the White Bear Reserve.

Below: Vest made of black cloth with a fabric back. The floral beadwork on the front suggests it was likely made by the Saulteaux, with bifurcated stems, four-petal rose, and smaller designs than those of the Minnesota Ojibwa. Vests, gloves, etc., were adopted by Indians during the 19th century.

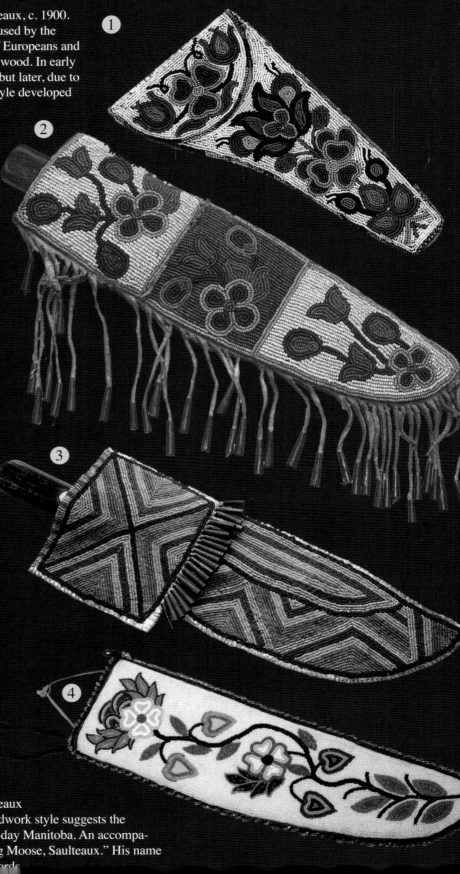

1 Beaded holster, probably Canadian Saulteaux, c. 1900. Semirealistic and floral designs have been used by the Ojibwa probably since before the arrival of Europeans and were engraved on birchbark and carved on wood. In early work delicate floral patterns predominated but later, due to European influences, a new semirealistic style developed around 1880, with large leaves and flowers designed to fill in large spaces on the front of bandoliers. Some repeating designs used birchbark or paper cutouts which were kept by the beadworker for future reference. Sometimes patterns were worked out with flour and water tracing the outline. The origin of cutout patterns is thought to go back to a time before modern implements for scoring were available, when Ojibwa women marked their designs with their teeth on birchbark.

2 Buckskin knife case with floral beaded designs and fringe of buckskin with tin cone jingles.

3 Rawhide knife case, solid beaded front in geometric designs. Probably Plains Ojibwa or Plains Cree, c. 1890. Mark Sykes Collection.

4 Knife case, Ojibwa (Chippewa), c. 1895. Worn as ceremonial regalia, it is constructed with velvet cloth, silk edge, and beadwork. The beadwork is typical late 19th century thread-sewn floralistic style of the Ojibwa (Chippewa) of Minnesota, Wisconsin, and adjacent Canada. When used with a knife, an inside rawhide or bark sheath would be used.

5 Two late 18th/early 19th century knife cases with porcupine quillwork decoration. This type was usually worn around the neck. See plate A1 on p. 98 and photo on p. 37.

6 Man's beaded cape worn during dances, c. 1910. Similar capes or "yokes" were worn by women.

7 Beaded vest or waistcoat, probably Saulteaux (Canadian Ojibwa), c. 1890. The floral beadwork style suggests the vest was from the Interlake area of present-day Manitoba. An accompanying note claims the vest "belonged to Big Moose, Saulteaux." His name appears in the Hudson's Bay Company records.

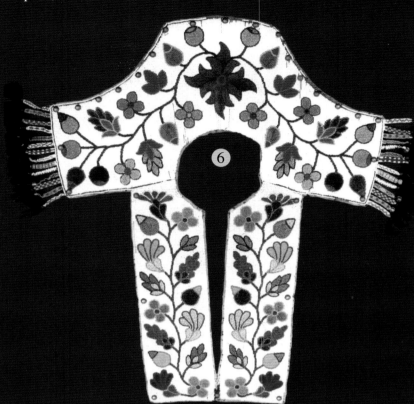

8 Ojibwa knife case of cloth and buckskin, c. 1890. The front is covered with woven bead-work and fringed with large beads and woolen tassels. Mark Sykes Collection.

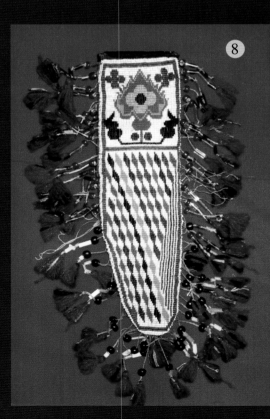

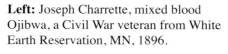

Left: Joseph Charrette, mixed blood Ojibwa, a Civil War veteran from White Earth Reservation, MN, 1896.

Right: Kis-ki-ta-wag, Ojibwa, c. 1880. He wears a woven beaded bandolier bag, and holds a porcupine-quilled pipe stem.

Below Left: Sampson White Pigeon and Reuben Young, Potawatomi, near Arpin, Wisconsin, 1915.

Below Right: Ojibwa man, Midwewining (One Called From a Distance), 1894. He holds an iron pipe tomahawk, and wears a woven beaded bandolier in geometric designs and an appliqué beaded panel on his chest. He also wears a head roach (porcupine hair) and turban.

Below: Man, probably Ojibwa, c. 1910. His bandolier bags, apron, and moccasins suggest they were made by the Winnebago people. The tabs and offset at the junction of the shoulder strap and bag are Winnebago traits.

Left and Below Left: An Ojibwa man's dance shirt of the period 1890–1920. It consists of a hand-made green-colored cotton cloth shirt of ordinary Euro-American style with added panels of black velveteen decorated with floral Ojibwa-style bead-work. There are two fitted panels to the front, a rectangular panel on the shoulder, and two truncated rectangular cuffs to the sleeves. The basic shirt construction appears to have been made with an old hand-cranked sewing machine, whereas the beaded panels are attached by hand sewing. The beadwork is typical Wisconsin and Minnesota Ojibwa work of the period, that being the spot or appliqué sewn work using two threads, one to string the beads and the other sewn down on the velveteen.

Below: Man's cloth hood with ears. Ojibwa or Cree, early 19th century. Perhaps used as a hunting aid or in rituals to attract game. The artist Rindisbacher pictured a hunter shooting a bison wearing a hood with double ears, made of colored cloth, c. 1822, near the Red River Settlement. Royal Ontario Museum.

Opposite, Above: Ojibwa men photographed in Washington in 1911. The men wear typical ritual attire of the period. Headdresses include a roach, fur turban, and buffalo-horned types. They hold iron tomahawks, a gunstock war club, and a pipe.

Opposite, Below Left: Ah-ah-shaw-we-ke-shick (Crossing Sky), Chief of the Rabbit Lake Ojibwa, 1869. He wears an early-style woven beaded bandolier bag. Photograph: Whitney Gallery, St. Paul, MN.

Opposite, Below Right: Group of Ojibwa in festive attire at Grand Portage, MN, c. 1920. Man left front holds a hand drum with painted symbols.

Left: Edawigijig (Both Sides of the Sky) is of the Bad River Ojibwa, who signed the Treaty of 1854, with a woven beaded bandolier bag and peace medal, c. 1874.

Below: Ojibwa group, Bois Forte Band, MN, c. 1900. Boy wears floral beaded vest and apron. The older man holds an iron pipe tomahawk and rifle with metal studs. He wears skunk garters, the badge of a former warrior. Behind is a gabled wigwam constructed with what appears to be elm bark slabs.

Above: Delegation of Ojibwa men from Red Lake Reservation to Washington D.C. in 1909.

Right: George Sky (Thunder Sky), Lac du Flambeau, Ojibwa, 1924. He holds a large carved pipe stem. His beaded harness has the letters "SKY, LDF, WIS" his name, reservation, and state initials.

Far Right: The Round Earth, Ojibwa delegate to Washington D.C., 1908. He wears a heavily beaded pair of leggings, two bandoliers, and a belt.

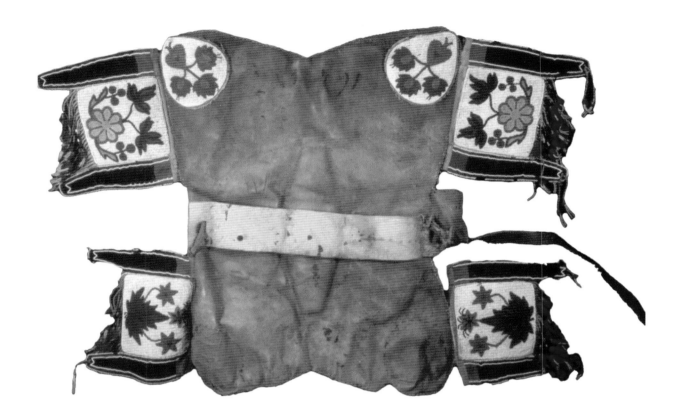

Above: Beadwork decoration could be found on Hide pad saddle, probably Plains Ojibwa or Métis, c. 1880. Beaded tabs and corners.

Left: Pad saddle, buckskin and heavy canvas, filled with deer hair, c. 1900. Embroidered with thread-couched overlay beadwork. Many similar saddles have been reported as Métis but there is nothing to suggest any difference from Plains Ojibwa make. Courtesy Richard Green.

EAGLE FEATHER HEADDRESSES

The Ojibwa used eagle feathers to signify war honors and chieftainship. They did not wear them unless they had been awarded for war exploits, particularly bravery. It has been suggested one was worn for each enemy scalp taken and their decoration with a red spot indicated the wearer had been wounded by a bullet. If the feather was split, this, too, indicated that the wearer had been wounded. A number of feathers fixed upright gave evidence of the number of scalps taken. Other headdresses have feathers at the back of the head or side, and when worn horizontally at the front of the head indicated times of peace. Hawk and wild turkey feathers were also sometimes used.

Above and Below Left: Ojibwa man, photographed in Washington D.C. in 1899, wearing a bear claw necklace and beaded accessories in floral designs: a belt, pouch, knife sheath, and shirt strips. The fur garters, which appear to be skunk, may indicate his former status as a warrior.

Above Right: Ojibwa "Chief" Thomas Obtossaway (c. 1903), a participant in a pageant based on Henry Wadsworth Longfellow's "Song of Hiawatha" first held at Desbarats, Ontario, in 1900. He was probably from Sucker Creek Reserve, Manitoulin Island — near Little Current — where his brother was chief.

Right: Ojibwa man, c. 1900, wearing beaded vest, braided yarn or wool turban, and loop necklace. Wearing feathers horizontally on the head was a typical Ojibwa style.

Opposite: J-aw-beance, an Ojibwa (Chippeway) chief, wearing a medallion and a feathered headdress. From a painting attributed to Charles Bird King, but not included in McKenney and Hall (1933).

Opposite, Inset: Moosehair band mounted with a strip of woven porcupine quillwork worked with sinew thread in a geometric pattern. The two ends enjoined with quill-wrapped thongs at back. Upright dyed hair fitted inside band. Collected by Nicholas Cresswell, c. 1775.

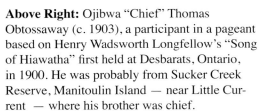

Painted by C. B. King

Lehman & Duval Lith'rs Philad.a

Arrowmaker, a participant in a Hiawatha play
(see Obtossaway caption on p. 94), c. 1903.
Probably Garden River Ontario. The beadwork on
his jacket and necklace is not Woodland Ojibwa;
however, the horizontally tied feathers in his hair
was considered a warrior custom, but used in
times of peace by Ojibwa men.

Far Left: Chief Buffalo, photographed c. 1862, was possibly a relative of the famous Chief Buffalo at La Pointe, WI, who died in 1855. He wears a braided sash around his waist and turkey feathers on his top hat.

Left: Wingard, Ojibwa, holding an iron pipe tomahawk, c. 1908. Note the positions and arrangement of the eagle feathers in his turban, which could indicate his status as a former warrior.

Below: Ojibwa (Chippewa) men, c. 1910–1920, perhaps a singing group at a powwow. The men wear floral beaded shirts and the man on the right wears floral beaded leggings as well. These items and moccasins appear to be Ojibwa-made; however, the feather head-dresses and leggings of the center men are adopted Plains regalia.

PLATE A

A1   A2   A3

PLATE B

B1

B2

B3

PLATE C

C1

C2

C3

PLATE A

A1 This man's attire is based upon material collected by Andrew Foster, a lieutenant in the British Army, at Fort Michilimackinac, Lake Michigan, c. 1780. The headdress is of eagle tail feathers with quillwork on the spines and horsehair on a cloth band decorated with metal rings. He wears silver earrings, a quilled neck knife case, a woven yarn or fiber belt sash with quilled belt pouch, and holds another quill-decorated pouch with knife. His shirt was obtained from white traders and has metal or silver rings sewn on. The blue trade-cloth leggings would be held by thongs at the waist and by fringed garters at the knee. His moccasins are the one-piece center-seam type, possibly with a gore covered with quillwork. The actual items collected by Foster were probably from a number of different tribes who visited the fort. The collection is now in the National Museum of the American Indian.

A2 Northern Ojibwa Subarctic hunter, c. 1800. His attire is dominated by a moose-hide coat, one of a number of examples that survive in museums. This one is based upon a specimen in the National Museums of Scotland, Edinburgh. The genesis of these "coats" was no doubt whole wraparound moose or caribou-hide body covers for protection against the severe weather. The fur trade had already introduced European influences, perhaps the front opening and sleeves, by the late 17th century, and subsequently refinements to the collar, cuffs, and fitting during the period 1750–1850. As the Ojibwa moved north they probably adopted this form from the Crees. The early coats are painted with geometric and curvilinear designs in horizontal, vertical, and border bands of blues, reds, and yellows; later in floral painted and quilled designs. The later versions were often attributed to the Red River Métis. The coat is also decorated with woven quilled bands at the shoulders and the symmetry of the painted designs suggests the use of in-struments. He also has a porcupine-quilled three-sectioned shoulder pouch and wears skin leggings and moccasins. He holds a hatchet with an iron pipe-tomahawk head obtained in trade.

A3 Ojibwa mother and baby, mid-19th century. The Ojibwa wooden cradle was a flat-back board with a curved head bow, which gave some protection to the infant and from which charms were suspended. The top of the board has carved designs. The Southern Ojibwa has a wraparound wide cloth to secure the baby. By this period women's dress has become Americanized but decorated with ribbon on both skirt and knee-length leggings. Moccasins, with U-shaped cloth vamps and cloth collars, were decorated with beadwork and ribbons.

PLATE B

B1 Ojibwa woman in formal attire, c. 1885. She wears a cloth hood with ribbon and beadwork. Her velveteen type dress is Euro-American in style with the skirt heavily beaded with floral designs and bodice with beaded panels. Her leggings are knee height trade cloth, beaded, with ribbon trimming. Her belt is solid beading and she holds a cloth bag. She wears a fine bandolier bag on her left shoulder over to her right hip. The bandolier is woven and beaded in traditional geometric patterns with tassels along the bottom edge. The buckskin moccasins are the typical later Ojibwa type with the instep covered with a cloth "vamp" decorated with beaded floral designs.

B2 Minnesota Ojibwa man in full dress, c. 1895. The arrangement of eagle feathers on a fur fillet or braided yard head-dress was the mark of a former warrior. The development of floral beadwork reached a zenith among the Ojibwa of Minnesota and Wisconsin during the last two decades of the 19th century. Parts of the man's attire are known to have come from Leech Lake Reservation in Minnesota: the shirt (with a U-shaped velveteen chest panel), trade cloth leggings, aprons, and bandolier. The use of black material as a background probably descends from the former use of black-dyed buckskin. He holds a ball-headed club and tobacco bag.

B3 Plains Ojibwa man, c. 1890. The regalia worn by this man reflect the influences of the Northern Plains. The shirt is one of a number in a similar genre, of trade cloth, with beaded strips and roundels.

Photographs of two men wearing this example (one from Turtle Mountain, ND) are known. The shirt is now in the Plains Indian Museum, Browning, MT. He wears cloth leggings with geometric beaded designs, aprons with floral beaded designs (collected in Saskatchewan), separate-soled moccasins, and holds up a brass-studded dance quirt and fur stole, perhaps a society badge.

PLATE C

C1 Ojibwa Grass Dancer, c. 1958. Based on Grass Dance regalia from Saskatchewan and a champion dancer of the 1950s from Turtle Mountain Reservation, ND. He wears a basic cloth shirt and leggings or trousers with V-shaped fringing on either leg in front. Beaded rosettes with tassels orna-ment the shirt and trousers. He also wears a beaded collar and tie, arm bands, gauntlets, head band, and belts. A large porcupine and deer roach with two downy plumes attached to automobile choke-spring wire is worn on the head. These "antennae" bounce grace-fully with the dancer's movements.

C2 Jingle-dress dancer, Ojibwa, 1990s. Both the Plains and Woodland Ojibwa claim the earliest form of dark cloth dresses decorated with rows of tin cones that give a jingling sound when dancing. Older dresses are solid-color cloth, later ones are multi-colored. Some quasi-religious current beliefs suggest instructions to make these dresses are connected with healing and dreams. This style of dress is now popular with all tribes and is a distinctly Ojibwa contribution to Pan-Indianism.

C3 Northern Ojibwa/Saulteaux fur trapper, c. 1900. The white man introduced the system of the exchange of European goods for the procurement of furs by the indigenous peoples of North America. Within a few years of the arrival of the Europeans eastern tribes became depen-dent upon their trade goods, such as guns, knives, and cloth. The Ojibwa spread far to the north and west to satisfy the demands of the fur trade companies until diminish-ing supply and demand by the 20th century. This northern hunter wears moose-hide mittens and has a firebag in his belt.

WOMEN'S CLOTHING

1 Eastern Ojibwa (Chippewa) woman photographed at Muncey Town, Thames River, Ontario, in 1907. Three small groups of Chippewa, Muncey-Delaware and Oneida-Iroquois have reserves south of London, Ontario. Although she is probably Chippewa, this lady wears a characteristically Iroquoian cloth dress, cape, skirt, and pouch. The same pouch also figures in a contemporaneous photograph of the Oneida Chief John Danford.

2 & 3 Early 20th century Ojibwa black cloth dresses profusely covered with floral beadwork.

4 Ojibwa girl with native crafts made for sale, including a model birchbark canoe and split-wood baskets. She has a woven beaded bandolier over her shoulders. Probably Lac Vieux Desert Band, northern Wisconsin/Michigan border, early 20th century.

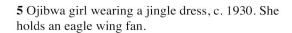

5 Ojibwa girl wearing a jingle dress, c. 1930. She holds an eagle wing fan.

6 Marie Louise Bottineau-Baldwin, mixed blood Ojibwa, 1914. Behind her is an example of Indian lace making that flourished in Minnesota until the 1920s. She was the first Native graduate from the Washington College of Law.

7 Potawatomi girl, holding a ribbonwork decorated blanket at the St. Louis World's Fair, 1904.

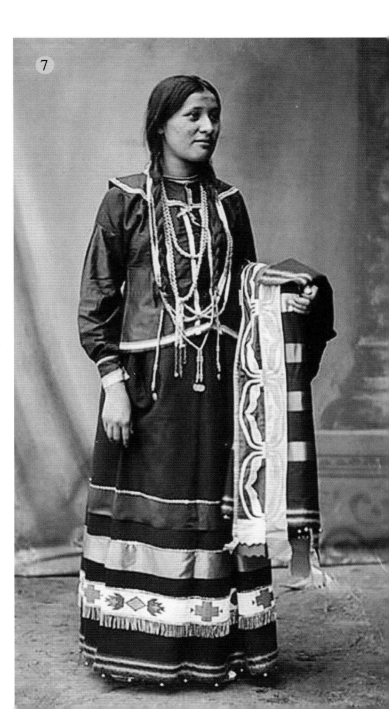

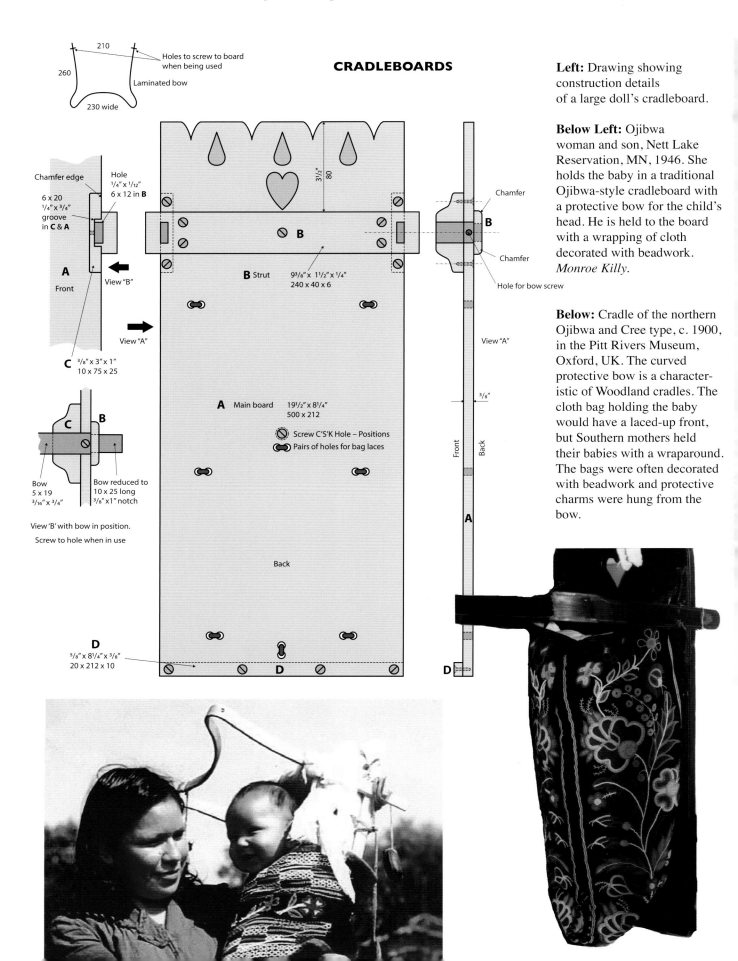

CRADLEBOARDS

210

260

230 wide

Holes to screw to board
when being used

Laminated bow

Chamfer edge

Hole
¼" x ¹⁄₁₂"
6 x 12 in **B**

6 x 20
¼" x ¾"
groove
in **C** & **A**

A

Front

View "B"

C ³⁄₈" x 3" x 1"
10 x 75 x 25

3½"
80

B

B Strut   9³⁄₈" x 1½" x ¼"
240 x 40 x 6

A Main board   19½" x 8¼"
500 x 212

⊘ Screw C'S'K Hole – Positions
Pairs of holes for bag laces

Back

C

B

Bow
5 x 19
³⁄₁₆" x ¾"

Bow reduced to
10 x 25 long
³⁄₈" x1" notch

View 'B' with bow in position.
Screw to hole when in use

D
⁵⁄₈" x 8¼" x ³⁄₈"
20 x 212 x 10

Chamfer

B

Chamfer

Hole for bow screw

View "A"

³⁄₈"

Front

Back

A

D

Left: Drawing showing
construction details
of a large doll's cradleboard.

Below Left: Ojibwa
woman and son, Nett Lake
Reservation, MN, 1946. She
holds the baby in a traditional
Ojibwa-style cradleboard with
a protective bow for the child's
head. He is held to the board
with a wrapping of cloth
decorated with beadwork.
Monroe Killy.

Below: Cradle of the northern
Ojibwa and Cree type, c. 1900,
in the Pitt Rivers Museum,
Oxford, UK. The curved
protective bow is a characteristic of Woodland cradles. The
cloth bag holding the baby
would have a laced-up front,
but Southern mothers held
their babies with a wraparound.
The bags were often decorated
with beadwork and protective
charms were hung from the
bow.

Above: Minnesota Ojibwa woman holding a child in a cradle-board, c. 1913. The child is held in position by a wraparound band of broadcloth decorated with fine floral beadwork.

Above Right: Baby in cradleboard, Saulteaux Grassy Narrows Band (English River), Ontario, early 20th century.

Right: Ojibwa woman and child, Minnesota, c. 1900. Note the cradleboard with a protective curved bow and beaded cloth wrapping; also, the wigwam frame behind.

BAGS AND POUCHES

To survive in a world filled with potentially dangerous supernatural power, hunters and warriors needed to acquire the protection of a personal guardian manito usually obtained via visionary experiences through a series of fasts and bodily deprivations. The visions became the origin of many motifs that were embroidered into personal clothing and possessions, or used in body paint. Such ornaments were worn at rituals and regarded as imbued with the manito's power.

These representations were frequently embroidered on pouches and bags worn by hunters and warriors. They were containers for tobacco, personal medicines, and implements used for firearms. Around the end of the 18th century a number of pouches that have survived were made of black-dyed deerskin; sometimes a belt pouch or a pouch with a shoulder strap. These are usually divided into sections — a strap, a central panel divided into horizontal quilled sections including a lower area decorated with underwater panthers or thunderbirds. Another form of pouch was the bag woven from natural fibers used as containers for medicine objects with supernatural power. These bags also display depictions of thunderbirds and underwater panthers, often also in three design zones which correspond to the three levels of the universe — the sky world, the middle realm of the earth, and the underworld. Not all woven bags display images of manitos; some have geometrical designs perhaps intended to express energy or power lines with interwoven wampum or trade bead designs.

As contacts and trade with white people increased, European commodities began to replace native materials which reflected in new forms of pouches and bags made with burlap and trade cloth and decorated with large panels of woven yarn with interspaced beads or later of seed beadwork. Later so-called bandolier bags probably are derived from a combination of these older native fiber and buckskin pouches decorated with paint and porcupine quills with Euro-American frontiersmen's ammunition bags.

Above: Some examples of Ojibwa iconography in porcupine quill-work in this c. 1830 item from the Field Museum of Natural History, Chicago, IL. Note the church, ship, and turtles.

Right: Eleven woven beaded tabs and woolen tassels attached to the lower edge of the main beaded area of a bandolier bag. One tab appears to be a miniature U.S. flag design.

These resulting beaded bags became an essential part of ceremonial costume for men and sometimes women during the second half of the 19th century, particularly when worn for the Dream Dance and Mide rituals. They were also known as Friendship Bags and given as gifts to visitors. The Sioux would trade horses for them. Almost none of the hundreds of bags that have survived have any recorded history, but many are known to have come from the reservations of Lac du Flambeau and Lac Courte Oreilles in Wisconsin and Red Lake, White Earth, Leech Lake, and Mille Lacs in Minnesota and the reserves along Rainy River and Lake of the Woods in Ontario. Other tribes such as the Menominee, Potawatomi, Winnebago, and Sauk also made bandoliers, but few if any from the Ottawa.

The Ojibwa made by far the largest number of bandolier bags and many survive in museums, private collections, and among Indian families. Early bags (1850–1880) were usually woven and beaded using a wooden box frame for the warps with designs in traditional geometrical patterns, then quite suddenly there was a switch to floral designs (1880–1920) with beadwork in appliqué technique using two threads: one to thread the beads, the other to sew them down. The bag form was often quite similar; in three parts, a shoulder strap, a central panel usually only partly beaded, and a fully beaded bag panel — perhaps repeating the form of much earlier bags. By about 1850 Euro-American materials such as broadcloth and cotton thread had replaced native buckskin and sinew for ceremonial clothing and bandoliers utilized trade cloth, sackcloth, velvet, velveteen, wool, twill tape, printed cotton, woolen tassels, and a vast range of seed beads of various colors.

The origin and spread of realistic floral designs among the North American Indians is complex, but briefly combines an existing native curvilinear art tradition with European folk art which arrived in the New World with the French along the St. Lawrence River and the British on Hudson and James bays and spread with the advancing fur trade and missions.

Ojibwa seed beadwork displays maple and oak leaves, grapes, wild plant leaves, printed fabrics often with interconnecting vines, buds and leaves of unrelated plants. Each bag was created in difficult circumstances — often severe poverty and deprivation — which was a feature of early reservation life, particularly during the period most of these examples were made (1875–1910). Each bag displays the skill, care, and artistically arranged components required and communicates much about the women who made them during a time when many Ojibwa still lived in bark lodges in summer and ramshackle dwellings in winter.

Some of the later bandoliers (c.1900–1930) actually have no bags, simply a large beaded front panel, or a small "letterbox" slit as an opening. These were just a part of ceremonial attire. By about 1930 the older generation of skilled bead workers had gone and since then few bandoliers have been made.

Above: Ojibwa man wearing crossed bandolier bags and beaded cloth leggings, apron, and vest. Probably photographed at Long Lake, Wisconsin c. 1913.

Below: Bandolier bag with access to the bag section by means of a small slit often called a letterbox. Completely covered with floral beadwork except for woven beaded tabs; probably c. 1920. *Courtesy Wayne Wagner Collection.*

PANEL BAGS

This was a general type of 18th century pouch consisting of a buckskin upper, painted or dyed, with a lower fringe of quill-wrapped thongs. During the 19th century this style became a cloth upper bag section with a rounded top and a lower woven beaded panel and beaded fringe. The bag was usually beaded front and back with floral designs and the panel in geometric patterns. A number of this type of pouch are associated with James Bay Cree (**1**) and Red River Métis (**2**). Mark Sykes Collection.

3 An older type of bag originally of skin or woven fiber with horizontal bands of quillwork dividing the pouch into at least three distinct areas at the front. Adding a shoulder strap (probably a European trait) this could be the precursor of the bandolier bag of the Southwestern Ojibwa popular after about 1850.

4 Shoulder pouch of finger-woven fiber or yarn with a band of quillwork, and interwoven beads in the design of a thunderbird with three heads. Probably Ojibwa or Odawa, early 19th century, item photographed in the National Museums of Scotland.

5 Among the earliest-known survivors of the pouches of the Algonkians of the western Great Lakes are a number that are trapezoidal-shaped of black-dyed buckskin. These feature either geometrical or representational quilled designs from native cosmology, such as thunderbirds and underwater panthers, and are usually about 10 to 12 in. (24–30 cm) long and 4 to 6 in. (10–15 cm) wide. These depictions are of the powerful supernatural beings of the upper world and underworld of the native cosmos.

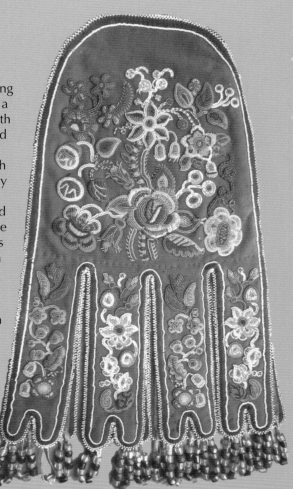

OCTOPUS BAGS

Octopus bags or pouches — usually with four pairs of hanging tabs — probably descend from a type of animal skin pouches with hanging legs that were recorded by artist John Smith among the Carolina Algonkians in the 16th century. A few rare 18th century bags with two or three hanging tabs survive made of black-dyed skin or painted buckskin. By the mid-19th century this form was constructed of trade cloth with beaded tassels and fringing, and a rounded top, usually beaded with floral designs. They are associated first with James Bay Cree, then with the Ojibwa and Métis of Manitoba. Subsequently this type spread north and west, to the Athabascan peoples, then to the Northwest coast and Plateau by the end of the 19th century.

Left and Right: Both sides of an Octopus or four-tab pouch of dark trade cloth, floral beadwork, and wool tassels. Beadwork design details suggest that it was made in the Lake Winnipeg area, Canadian Ojibwa (Saulteaux) and c. 1880. Today it is in the Canadian Museum of History, Gatineau, Quebec.

Opposite, Left: Four-tab pouch, c. 1880, of dark broadcloth with floral beadwork, probably Métis. *Courtesy Mark Sykes.*

Opposite, Right: Octopus pouch of cloth with floral beadwork, probably Red River Métis, c. 1880. The beadwork designs are the confluence of Ojibwa, Cree, and French-Canadian influences. *Courtesy Mark Sykes.*

Left: Ojibwa (Saulteaux) couple, Little Grand Rapids Band, east coast Lake Winnipeg, c. 1935. The man is wearing an octopus bag around his neck.

Below: Beadwork detail from a late 19th century Octopus bag attributed to the Métis. The central rose design appears to be of British influence to the mix of floral patterns used by Cree, Ojibwa, and Métis beadworkers of the Subarctic and Woodlands.

BANDOLIER BAGS

These bags were sometimes known as friendship bags as they were often given away at tribal and intertribal gatherings. The Sioux frequently traded horses for them. The origins of such bags were probably the colonial soldiers' bullet pouches of the 18th century. They were adopted by the eastern Indians and decorated with quill-work or, later, beaded designs. They were used at one time to carry ammunition and food but later simply as an item of ceremonial dress worn by both men and women, usually diagonally across the chest. Wearing bandolier bags among the Ojibwa became an ethnic symbol at social and religious gatherings and often carried religious meaning. Many bandolier bags were made in the late 19th century by the Southern Ojibwa (also called Chippewa) at first in woven beadwork, later in appliqué sewn beadwork usually onto red or black cloth or velvet, with borders around the lower panels. Some very late bandoliers even lacked the opening or bags completely (see examples on p. 107 and on pp. 114, 115, 116). The bags with geometrically woven designs sometimes contained the X motif — probably stylized thunderbirds — and hence had religious overtones.

Woven beaded bandolier without bag. The bandolier is of the popular velveteen-backed construction. The narrow central section suggests Potawatomi origin, c. 1890.

Left: Ojibwa bandolier bag 15 in. (38 cm) wide by 45 in. (114 cm) long overall. The front panel and shoulder strap are beaded on canvas and cloth. The central panel and sides are in velveteen. Edging is in red tape and backed with patterned cloth. The words depicted in beadwork are "Lake Lena Minn" and dated 1917, probably indicating place and date of make. The main floral beaded panel in symmetrical designs developed from a lower-central five-lobed flower element.

Opposite
Left: Ojibwa bandolier, c. 1900. Appliqué beaded on burlap and velveteen. The zig-zag borders are a simplification of earlier designs.

Above Right: John Stillway, Leech Lake Ojibwa, 1913. He wears a head roach and crossed bandoliers with beaded floral designs.

Below Right: John Mink, a Lac Courte Oreilles Ojibwa photographed in 1941 wearing a "Lake Lena" bandolier bag dated 1930. Curiously there appear to be eleven tabs along the bottom edge similar to the other examples bearing the name Lake Lena in beads.

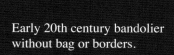

This bag is a composite of lower panel and shoulder strap, the lower panel of cloth and velveteen beaded in floral appliqué (two-thread). The shoulder strap or baldric is similarly beaded in pomegranate and leaf designs. The strap is reported to have been collected from the Red Thunder family of the Yanktonai Sioux but likely to have been made by Ojibwa beadworkers. The lower panel has "New Chippewa Walker, MN, Hackensack $148, c.1922. Paul" written in ink on the fabric. Early 20th century or before.

Large — 42 in. (107 cm) long — beaded shoulder bandolier without a bag, simply an item of regalia, c. 1910. Constructed of sacking, edged with velveteen and backed with cloth. The two narrow, partly beaded bands of velveteen between the shoulder baldric and lower panel suggests Potawatomi make, as does the less fluid floral patterns.

Early 20th century bandolier without bag or borders.

Bandolier bag of old red trade cloth with selvedged edge. The beadwork is loom-woven, except the borders, in stylized geometrical and floral designs with the X motifs on the shoulder straps probably representing thunderbirds. The bag probably dates to c. 1880.

Bandolier made without a pocket or bag, of canvas or sacking lined with cloth and sewn with floral beadwork. A late form of bandolier, c. 1920, 43 in. (109 cm) long.

Bandolier bag of heavy cloth and lined. The bag is in the typical three sections, shoulder strap, narrow partly beaded middle section, and lower large panel. The lower panel of woven beadwork is a fine example of the generalized X motif thought to be derived from the representation of the thunderbird of Woodland mythology. The bag dates to c. 1885.

Bandolier bag, heavy cloth, lined and beaded in floral designs. There is no middle section, instead it has a letterbox opening to the bag (lower) section, characteristic of a number of bandolier bags of the period 1890–1920, as are the tassels along the lower edge on almost all bandoliers.

The borders on some Ojibwa beaded items use simple diamond designs which occur in conjunction with elongated hexagons to represent the tracks of the sacred otter, or specifically his tail in the snow — as here and at right. Dating to c. 1875–1885, probably from Wisconsin, this bag — 10 in. (25 cm) wide by 44 in. (112 cm) long — is made of cloth, velvet, military braid, and beadwork. These woven beaded bags were popular until about 1885; afterwards, appliqué beaded floral designs predominated.

Lovely example of 19th century Woodlands beadwork with a floral design showing great skill at color combination. The lower part of the bag has a white bead edging that is reminiscent of lace. The back of the shoulder strap is navy and white cotton cloth. The lower portion of the bag is backed by black velvet. The tassels are made of cut-glass beads and yarn. In excellent condition, by far one of the most beautiful examples we have seen. No restoration. 12¾ in. (32 cm) wide by 43 in. (109 cm) long.

Typical Ojibwa bandolier bag of wool cloth, with military braid edging, yarn tassels, and beads. The floral beading is typical of the 1880–1910 period. The beaded border to the lower area is sometimes called "otter-tail" design. Some of the beadwork uses cut beads. The small design elements suggest possibly a Canadian Ojibwa attribution. Bag length 16 in. (12 cm); width 10 in. (25 cm); strap 48 in. (122 cm) long; width 5 in. (12 cm).

Bandolier bag from Red Lake. MN, c. 1900.

Bandolier without a bag, probably Wisconsin Potawatomi, c. 1890. Cloth backing for woven beaded front panel and strap with a woven beaded band between. The bandolier has tabs and tassels. The basic thunderbird and lightning designs and other figures preserve traditional lore.

FIRE BAGS, TOBACCO BAGS, AND PIPE BAGS

There are various names for these pouches made to contain tobacco and pipe for personal or ritual use. The common form of the second half of the 19th century for Plains Ojibwa, Plains Cree, and other Northern Plains peoples consisted of three parts: a buckskin upper section, a beaded section, and a lower fringed section. Although floral designs predominated the beaded area, often on both sides, geometric designs were also used. Many defy tribal attribution but several show Ojibwa characteristics whereas others are likely Cree.

Right: Moosehide tobacco bag with variegated floral beadwork panels on both sides. Marginal Plains, either Ojibwa or Cree c.1890.

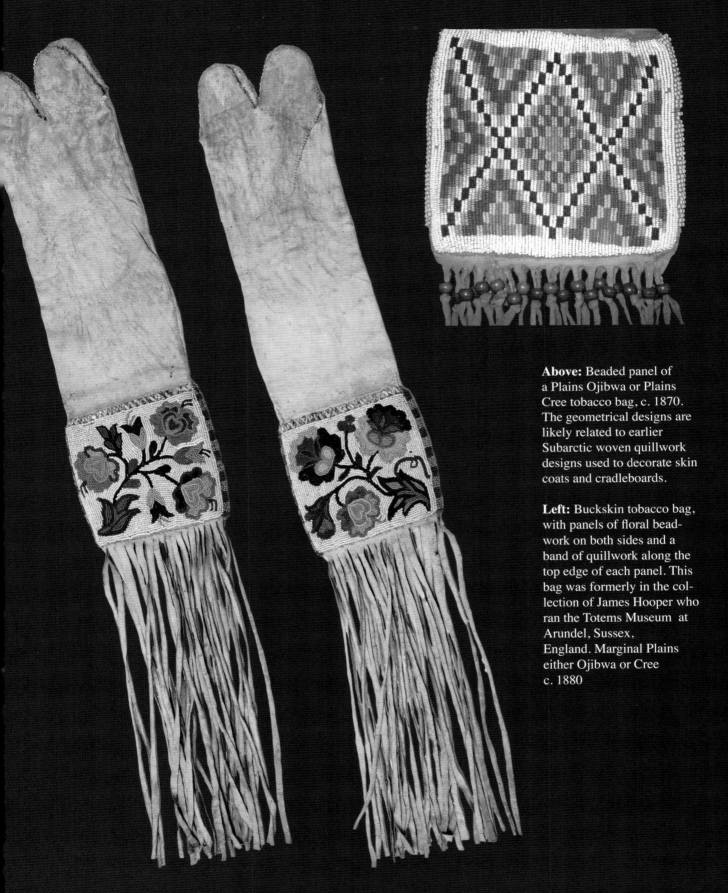

Above: Beaded panel of a Plains Ojibwa or Plains Cree tobacco bag, c. 1870. The geometrical designs are likely related to earlier Subarctic woven quillwork designs used to decorate skin coats and cradleboards.

Left: Buckskin tobacco bag, with panels of floral beadwork on both sides and a band of quillwork along the top edge of each panel. This bag was formerly in the collection of James Hooper who ran the Totems Museum at Arundel, Sussex, England. Marginal Plains either Ojibwa or Cree c. 1880

1 Beaded panels on two pipe bags or tobacco bags very probably from the Parklands or Canadian Plains, eastern Saskatchewan. It is difficult to determine if Ojibwa or Cree as they are mixed in this region. Both date c. 1870s.

2 Buckskin fire bag with panel of appliqué beaded floral designs. Probably Saulteaux or Plains Ojibwa, c. 1890. G. Messa Collection.

3 Three tobacco bags, also known as fire or pipe bags; two with buckskin upper parts and one cloth. Probably Plains Ojibwa or Plains Cree from southern Manitoba or southeastern Saskatchewan. The stiff and tighter floral designs as compared with the Minnesota-Wisconsin Ojibwa forms together with central four or five-petal rose design distinguish the beadwork of this area from the Woodland Ojibwa, c. 1875–1900.

4 Detail of a Canadian Ojibwa fire bag or pipe bag, probably Saulteaux or Plains Ojibwa, c. 1890. Buckskin with rounded tabs at the top are a feature of these northern bags. Many of this type of bag were made in southern Manitoba and southeastern Saskatchewan by Ojibwa, Cree, and Métis. The dark blue stems linking the floral elements suggest an Ojibwa provenance. G. Messa Collection.

5 and 6 Two sides of a pipe bag or fire bag, c. 1900. The fringe is wrapped with porcupine quills.

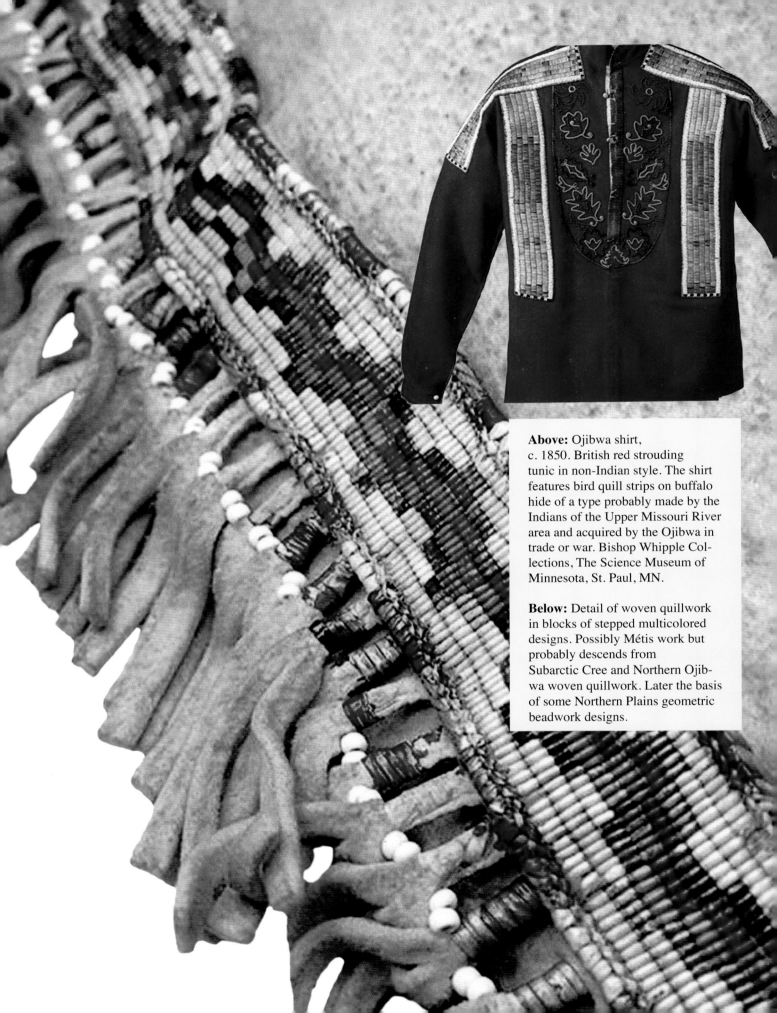

Above: Ojibwa shirt, c. 1850. British red strouding tunic in non-Indian style. The shirt features bird quill strips on buffalo hide of a type probably made by the Indians of the Upper Missouri River area and acquired by the Ojibwa in trade or war. Bishop Whipple Collections, The Science Museum of Minnesota, St. Paul, MN.

Below: Detail of woven quillwork in blocks of stepped multicolored designs. Possibly Métis work but probably descends from Subarctic Cree and Northern Ojibwa woven quillwork. Later the basis of some Northern Plains geometric beadwork designs.

QUILLWORK

Top Left: Birchbark tray decorated with porcupine quills, Ojibwa or Ottawa, early 20th century. *Minnesota Historical Society.*

Center Left: Selection of early, middle and late 20th century birchbark boxes decorated with colored porcupine quills. From Manitoulin Island, Ontario, and Michigan areas and either Ottawa or Ojibwa. *Vanessa Woods Collection.*

Bottom Left: Birchbark boxes decorated with porcupine quillwork. Top two early 20th century; bottom three, mid-20th century. Probably Odawa.

TYPICAL SCALLOPED QUILLED EDGE ON MANY MICHIGAN BARK BOXES

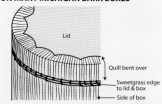

Lid

Quill bent over

Sweetgrass edge to lid & box

Side of box

TYPICAL LAYOUT OF QUILLS ON LID OF BARK BOX– FROM MANITOULIN ISLAND, CANADA

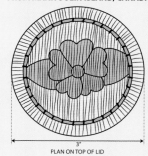

3"

PLAN ON TOP OF LID

TYPICAL "X" DESIGN AROUND RIM OF MANITOULIN ISLAND EXAMPLE OF QUILLED BOX

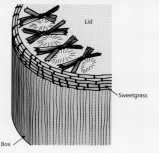

Lid

Sweetgrass

Box

MODERN CEREMONIAL DRESS

Below: Contemporary Grass Dancer at the George Gordon Powwow, Gordon Reserve, Saskatchewan. Although registered as a Plains Cree band many members are mixed Cree and Ojibwa. This man's regalia has matching beaded headband, cape, harness, and cuffs. *Leo Woods*.

Since the mid-1900s Ojibwa people (who now often spell their name Ojibwe) have revived interest in their cultural heritage, religion, crafts, painting, language, and celebrations. These so-called powwows, which are held on most reserves and reservations reflect the influences in song, dance and attire of the Plains but also many facets that are distinctly Ojibwa. This cultural mix is often referred to as Pan-Indianism.

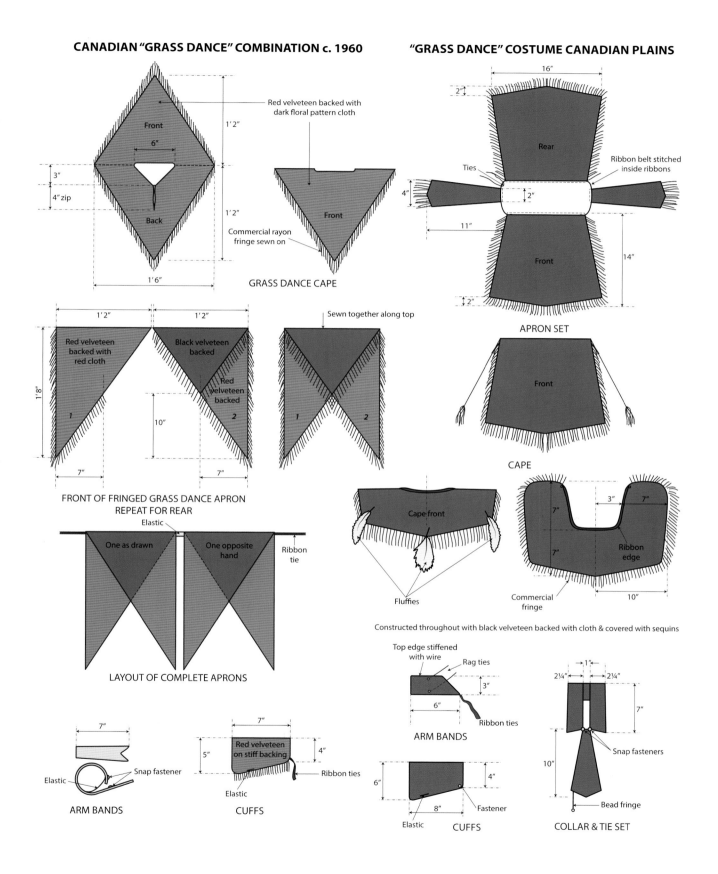

CANADIAN "GRASS DANCE" COMBINATION c. 1960

Red velveteen backed with dark floral pattern cloth

Front
6"
1'2"
3"
4" zip
Back
1'2"
1'6"

Commercial rayon fringe sewn on

Front

GRASS DANCE CAPE

Sewn together along top

1'2"   1'2"

Red velveteen backed with red cloth

Black velveteen backed

Red velveteen backed

1'8"

10"

1   2

7"   7"

1   2

FRONT OF FRINGED GRASS DANCE APRON
REPEAT FOR REAR

Elastic

One as drawn   One opposite hand

Ribbon tie

LAYOUT OF COMPLETE APRONS

7"

Snap fastener

Elastic

ARM BANDS

7"

Red velveteen on stiff backing

5"   4"

Ribbon ties

Elastic

CUFFS

"GRASS DANCE" COSTUME CANADIAN PLAINS

16"

2"

Rear

Ties

4"

2"

Ribbon belt stitched inside ribbons

11"

Front

14"

2"

APRON SET

Front

CAPE

Cape front

Fluffies

3"   7"

7"

7"   Ribbon edge

Commercial fringe   10"

Constructed throughout with black velveteen backed with cloth & covered with sequins

Top edge stiffened with wire

Rag ties

3"

6"

Ribbon ties

ARM BANDS

6"   4"

8"   Fastener

Elastic   CUFFS

2¼"   1"   2¼"

7"

10"

Snap fasteners

Bead fringe

COLLAR & TIE SET

Right: Turtle Mountain Plains Ojibwa Powwow in North Dakota, c. 1950. Men wearing bison horn and eagle feather headdresses. A woman wearing a cloth jingle dress with metal cones.

Below: Left, mastercraftsman Neil Oppendike, center Siobhan Marks at a Powwow in Wisconsin in Ojibwe attire. *Courtesy Charlie and Me Photography.*

Opposite, Above: Bear Creek Singers from Sault Ste. Marie.

Opposite, Below: Tribal Council of the Lac du Flambeau Band of Ojibwe in Wisconsin. Ojibwe is the preferred tribal spelling today.

Above Left: Girl singer at the Rama First Nations Powwow, Ontario.

Above Right: Lac Courte Oreilles, Ojibwa, dressed in beaded vest, leggings, apron, cuffs, arm bands, and porcupine and deer hair roach at a powwow in Madison, Wisconsin, in 2015. *Mike Rausch*.

Right: Red Lake Nation Independence Day Celebration, Minnesota, July 2015.

Far Right: Poster for Brokenhead Ojibway Nation Traditional Powwow, Manitoba, 2014.

Above: Girl dancers at the annual Mille Lacs Ojibwa Powwow in Minnesota.

Left: Kim Wheatly and daughter Alexandria Bipatnath, Ojibwa Shawanaga First Nation Reserve, Georgian Bay, Ontario. They wear their modern dance clothes with Turtle Clan designs on their shawls.

Chapter 5: People

Above: The Chief Andrew J. Blackbird House in Harbor Springs, MN, is listed on the National Register of Historic Places.

Banaise, Edward Benton (1934–) Ojibwa from Lac Courte Oreilles, WI. A qualified educator, teacher, and speaker of Midewiwin traditions, he has been influential in the revival and teaching of Ojibwa traditions to present-day tribal members. He is author of *The Mishomis Book: Voice of the Ojibwa* (Indian Country Press, St. Paul) and advisor to the Algoma University, a native university at Sault Ste. Marie.

Bizhiki (Buffalo or Great Buffalo) (c. 1759–1855) Ojibwa chief at La Pointe in modern northern Wisconsin and recognized leader of the Lake Superior Ojibwa (Chippewa), he signed treaties with the U.S. government in 1825, 1826, 1837, 1842, 1847, and 1854. He has often been confused with other Ojibwa contemporaries signing these treaties. He considered joining Tecumseh at Prophetstown in 1811 to take part in the attack on the Americans, but was convinced by the Métis fur trader Michel Cadotte that it would be pointless to fight the Americans. He sought peaceful tactics in relations with the U.S., but continued the traditional clashes with the Dakota. Buffalo's adopted son and interpreter, Benjamin Armstrong, describes a major victory for Buffalo's Ojibwa over a Dakota war party on the Brule River between La Pointe and Duluth in 1842, although historians have cast doubt on the validity of this account. He resisted attempts to move the Wisconsin bands to Minnesota after the Sandy Lake tragedy when many Ojibwa died attempting to obtain their annuities in Minnesota in 1850.

Blackbird, Andrew J. (c. 1815–1908) Ottawa (Odawa) of mixed descent, he attended white schools in eastern Michigan. Son of a chief, he served as an interpreter and official during treaty negotiations in 1855 that established Indian lands in the Harbor Springs area. Baptized a Catholic, he converted to Protestantism. His former home is now a museum. He wrote several books including *Complete Both Early and Late History of the Ottawa and Chippewa Indians of Michigan* (revised, Babcock and Darling, Harbor Springs, 1897).

Bug-o-na-ghe-zhisk or Po-go-nay-ge-shick (Hole in the Day II) (1825–1868) He inherited his father's position as chief of the Sandy Lake Ojibwa. Generally he adopted the manners and customs of the Americans but was mistrusted by both Indians and whites. Most likely killed by Pillager Ojibwas from the Leech Lake Reservation hired by mixed bloods from Crow Wing.

Chief Peguis (c. 1774–1864) Originally an Ojibwa from the Great Lakes, he moved first to Red Lake, MN, then to southern Manitoba about 1792. He ceded land to Lord Selkirk's settlers along the Red River in 1817. He converted to Christianity and was baptized William King. Pegius' son Mis-Koo-Kinew (Henry Prince) signed Treaty No. 1 in 1871. The present Pegius Band (several reserves) are located about 100 miles north of Winnipeg.

Curly Head (c. 1750–1825) Ojibwa chief, originally from the south shore of Lake Superior, he moved to the Crow Wing area of Minnesota. His warriors became a bulwark against the Dakota and he was always friendly with white traders. He met Lt. Zebulon Pike in 1805 and attended the Prairie du Chien Conference in 1825. He died while returning home.

Copway, George or Kahgegagahbowh (He Who Stands Forever) (1818–1869) Mississiauga Ojibwa, writer and Methodist missionary, he was born near Trenton, Ontario, into a traditional native family and converted to Methodism in 1827. He worked with missionaries in Wisconsin, was educated in Illinois, and ordained as a minister. He married Elizabeth Howell, an Englishwoman, and lived in Minnesota. Later he returned to Curve Lake and Saugeen reserves in Ontario, but was accused of embezzlement and defrocked. He wrote a best-selling memoir and history of the Ojibwa and ran an Indian newspaper for a time in New York. He recorded many details of birchbark scrolls that recorded details of Ojibwa history, rituals, and songs. He moved to Oka in Quebec in 1868 and converted to Catholicism; he died there the following year.

Densmore, Frances (1867–1957) Born in Red Wing, MN, she was an American ethnologist and musicologist. During the early 20th century she visited a number of "Chippewa" communities in Minnesota and Wisconsin, recording their culture and transcribing their songs. Working for the Smithsonian Institution's Bureau of American Ethnology she published reports with outstanding and invaluable information about a number of tribes (see photo overleaf).

Above: Chief Peguis memorial at Kildonan Park, Winnipeg.

Below: 1850 sketch of George Copway after Samuel Howell.

Flat Mouth I (c. 1774–1860) Chief of the Pillager Ojibwa around Leech Lake, MN, as a young warrior he took part in distant expeditions against tribes on the upper Missouri River, spending time amongst the Hidatsa. His band suffered at the hands of the Dakota. He was succeeded by his son of the same name, Flat Mouth II, who took part in a delegation to Washington D.C. in 1899.

Gauthier, Mrs. Benjamin (Double Sky Woman) Granddaughter of an Ojibwa leader of several Wisconsin bands, she visited Washington accompanying several tribal delegations. She lived at Lac du Flambeau, WI.

Hole-in-the-Day I (d. 1846) Succeeded Curly Head as war chief of the Sandy Lake Ojibwa in 1825. Agreed on a line of demarcation with their hereditary enemies, the Sioux, and the U.S. government in 1825. Much of his life was spent fighting the Sioux.

Johnston, Basil (1929–2015) Member of the Nawash First Nation (Cape Crocker Band), a revered author, ethnologist, and educator, he was predominantly concerned with the preservation of Ojibwa culture and lore. He worked for the Royal Ontario Museum for 25 years, traveled to lecture about Ojibwa history, and was a fluent native speaker.

Johnston, Jane (1800–1842) Ojibwa mixed blood, born Sault Ste. Mairie, MI, her mother was a daughter of a prominent chief and her father was John Johnston, a Scots-Irish fur trader born in Belfast. She married the Indian Agent and writer Henry Rowe Schoolcraft providing him with a unique understanding of Ojibwa culture and lore. They had four children.

Jones, Peter or Kahkewaquonaby or Sacred Feathers (1802–1856) Ojibwa Methodist minister, his mother was a Mississauga and his father a Welsh-born United Empire Loyalist. He was bilingual and bicultural. Elected chief of the New Credit Band, he obtained a new reserve from the Six Nations near Brantford, Ontario. He made several tours to England and had audiences with King William IV and, later, Queen Victoria at Windsor Castle in 1838. One of his five sons, Peter Edmund Jones (1843–1909), obtained a doctor's degree, became chief of the New Credit Band, and was involved in native politics. Despite being only one quarter Ojibwa, he refused to relinquish his Indian status.

Kegg, Maude (1904–1996) Ojibwa traditionalist, she was born into a community where cultural and religious beliefs still prevailed. She became a renowned informant for dictating native lore to students and scholars alike. She was a fine native artist and beadworker. She lived at the Mille Lacs Reservation, MN.

La Framboise, Madeline (c. 1780–1846) Of mixed French-Ottawa descent from the Grand River Band, she married Joseph La Framboise, a prominent fur trader. After her husband's death in 1806 she continued as a trader, supervising the movement of furs to Mackinac Island,

amassing a great fortune. She was later bought out by John Jacob Astor. Madeline spoke several languages but only began to learn to write in later life. Her daughter married Benjamin K. Pierce, brother of a future president of the U.S. Her later home is now a hotel at Mackinac Island. The lady called "Tshusick" painted in Washington by C.B. King in 1827 and published in McKenney and Hall, Vol. I., is often mistaken for her.

Langlade, Charles (1729–1802) Mixed blood, his mother was an Ottawa and his father a French fur trader. Born Mackinac, at age 10 he joined an Indian-French war party against the Chickasaws. He married first an Ottawa girl, but later remarried a daughter of an important French trader. In 1752 he led an Ottawa-Ojibwa war party against the Miami village of Pickawillany in Ohio. He was also reported to have been at Fort William Henry in 1755 and at Quebec in 1759. After the collapse of the Pontiac Rebellion of 1763 he moved to Green Bay and fought for the British side in the American Revolution. The Langlade-Grigon family became a prominent trading dynasty of Great Lakes Creoles, and are considered a major clan in the founding of the state of Wisconsin.

Matchekewis (c. 1735–1793) An Ojibwa warrior from Thunder Bay, he took part in the Pontiac Rebellion and the capture of Fort Michilimackinac in 1763. He fought for Britain during the Revolution, most notably at St. Louis in 1780 against the Spanish. He met Sir William Johnson (British Indian agent) and, later, De Peyster (British colonel) at Michilimackinac c. 1775.

Mokomaanish (?–1853) Ottawa (Odawa) war chief from Cross Village, Michigan, and ally of the British in the War of 1812. In 1815 he received the sword shown in the painting (on p. 134) from the British in recognition of his humanity towards a wounded American prisoner.

Opposite, from top:
Main-Ans (Little Wolf) with Francis Densmore in Washington D.C.

Mrs. Benjamin Gauthier in 1911.

Peter Jones.

Top: In 1780, during the American Revolution, the British and Indian forces made an unsuccessful attack on the town of St. Louis, whose then Spanish defenders had been assisting the Americans, see Matchekewis.

Below: Plaque at Green Bay remembering Charles Michel de Langlade and his father Augustin.

Morgan, Lewis Henry (1818–1881) Early American anthropologist and political and social theorist, Morgan graduated in 1840, and practiced law in Rochester, NY. He become interested in and an advocate for the New York Iroquois during their quest to regain their lands fraudulently obtained by the Ogden Land Company. Friend of Henry R. Schoolcraft and the Parker family of Tonawanda Senecas, his book *League of the Iroquois* was published in 1851, the result of cooperation with the Parker family. Later he became a successful businessman and traveled to visit several western tribes, including the Ojibwa, recording important data.

Okeemakeequid (The Chief that Speaks) Ojibwa. He is seen here (above left) in the painting by Charles Bird King for the three-volume *The Indian Tribes of North America* by McKenney and Hall, copied from an original painted by James Otto Lewis. Lewis accompanied McKenney and Lewis Cass to Fond du Lac to negotiate a treaty with the Vermilion Lake Band of "Chippeway" in 1826. The accuracy of Lewis' painting can be attested by the fur cape which survives in the collection of the Smithsonian Institution, Washington D.C. and is illustrated at left.

Okemos or John Okemos (c. 1775–1858) Saginaw Ojibwa from Michigan, he enlisted in the British Army in 1796. During the War of 1812 he fought against the Americans at the Battle of Fort Stephenson in Ohio. He represented the Saginaw Ojibwa at a meeting with Lewis Cass at the treaty with the U.S. in 1819.

Oshawana or John Naudee An Ojibwa warrior from Walpole Island he took part in Tecumseh's coalition, fighting against the Americans in the War of 1812. He participated in several battles including Frenchtown, Detroit, and Fort Meigs, supporting the British until the end of the war.

1 Okeemakeequid.

2 Mokomaanish.

3 John Okemos.

4 Okeemakeequid's fur cape.

5 Pontiac.

Peltier, Leonard (1944–) Native American political activist. His father was three quarters Ojibwa and his mother of Sioux extraction, born Grand Falls, ND, and lived his early life on Turtle Mountain Reservation and also in Seattle. Identified with native rights through the American Indian Movement (AIM) during factional disputes at Pine Ridge, SD, between traditionalists and corrupt tribal officials. Following violence in 1975 Peltier was subsequently arrested, and convicted in 1977 of the killing of two FBI agents despite inconsistent evidence. He remains in prison.

Pokagon, Leopold (c. 1775–1841) Potawatomi chief of the St. Joseph River Band in southern Michigan, he sought the help of the Catholic clergy to establish the formal identity of his band from earlier villages at Rush Lake, Dowagiac, and South Bend, IN. Present federally recognized Pokagon-Potawatomi lands are south of Kalamazoo, MI. His son, Simon Pokagon, was educated in Ohio and wrote a number of books and was welcomed by literary circles in Chicago and other cities. Nevertheless, he died in poverty in 1899.

Pontiac (c. 1720–1769) Ottawa chief. Probably born on the Maumee, OH. His father was most llikely Ottawa and his mother Ojibwa. He became noted for his role in the war against the British that followed their victory in the French and Indian War (1754–1760). The British had stopped distributing trade goods and presents that the Great Lakes Indians had come to rely on. The war began after a coalition of tribes sent 900 warriors to take Fort Detroit in 1763. A number of small forts were taken including Forts St. Joseph, Miami, Sandusky, Michilimackinac, and Ouiatenon; Fort Pitt was besieged but not taken. The following year the British launched two military expeditions, one under Col. John Bradstreet to relieve Detroit and the other under Col. Henry Bouquet to relieve Fort Pitt. This essentially ended the conflict. In 1766, Pontiac concluded a peace treaty with Sir William Johnson at Fort Ontario, NY. During the period of the conflict thousands of Indians died from smallpox, some say introduced by the British via infected trade goods. Pontiac was murdered in Illinois Country in 1769.

6 John Naudee.

7 FBI Wanted notice for Leonard Peltier.

Above: Rocky Boy.

Inset, Right: Henry Schoolcraft.

Rocky Boy or Stone Child (c. 1852–1916) Plains Ojibwa. He became leader of the landless Ojibwa of Montana after the death of Little Shell in 1901. In 1916 the Rocky Boy Reservation was established as a home for Ojibwa from various reservations, and for Little Bear's Crees from Canada. Little Bear (c. 1850–1921) was the son of Big Bear who had joined the Métis in the Northwest Rebellion in Canada in 1885.

Sagaunash or Billy Caldwell (c. 1780–1841) Son of William Caldwell, a Scots-Irish officer with Lord Dunmore (fighting the Shawnee in 1774 and serving with Butler's Rangers in the Revolutionary War), and a Mohawk girl (some say a Potawatomi), Sagaunash served the British cause until about 1820 when he moved to the Chicago area and was appointed a Potawatomi chief by the mixed bloods and white traders. He died near Council Bluffs, IA, in 1841. The name "Caldwell Band" is the only separate Potawatomi band registered in Canada today — although it lives mostly in the greater Detroit area, it is originally from Point Pelée, Ontario. However, any connection with Sagaunash is almost certainly incorrect, and the band has probably mixed Ojibwa and Potawatomi antecedents.

Sassaba (d. 1822) An Ojibwa warrior with Tecumseh during the War of 1812, he lost a brother at the Battle of the Thames which embittered Sassaba against the Americans. He refused to negotiate with Lewis Cass at Sault Ste. Marie in 1820, hoisting a British flag over his tent and dressed in a British military coat. He was drowned with his wife and child in 1822.

Schoolcraft, Henry Rowe (1783–1864) Noted for his important early studies of American Indian cultures, Schoolcraft joined Lewis Cass on an expedition to explore the upper Mississippi region in 1820; his second expedition in 1832 found its source at Lake Itasca. He married Jane Johnston, a mixed blood Ojibwa and was U.S. Indian Agent at Sault Ste. Marie. Between 1851 and 1857 he produced in six volumes, *Historical and Statistical Information, Respecting the History, Condition, and Prospects of the Indian Tribes of the United States*, with illustrations by Capt. Seth Eastman, published by Congress.

Shabeni (d. 1859) Born an Ottawa, he was chief of a Potawatomi village when he met Tecumseh in 1808 and became a devoted follower of the Shawnee chief. He provided Nehemiah Matson details of Tecumseh's unsuccessful sojourn to the Wisconsin tribes in 1810 to enlist their support against the U.S. He lived in Illinois after the War of 1812 and died near Morris dependent upon the charity of local white friends.

Shingabawassin (Reclining Human Figure of Stone) (c. 1763–c. 1830) Ojibwa leader from the St. Mary's River region of Michigan, he took an active part in war expeditions against the Sioux but was later a strong advocate for peace. He was present at the councils for the treaties at Prairie du Chien 1825, and Fond du Lac in 1826. His portrait of 1826 by J.O. Lewis, painted at Fond du Lac, was copied by C.B. King for McKenney and Hall, Vol 1.

Sitting White Eagle (b. 1840–?) Plains Ojibwa. His father was a Plains Ojibwa and his mother a Swampy Cree and part of the Peguis Ojibwa band of Manitoba. After the sale of land to Lord Selkirk to establish the Red River settlement in 1817, the family moved southwest onto the buffalo plains. During his lifetime he was in five battles with the Sioux, and many with the Blackfoot and Crows. He later lived on the Sakimay Reserve in the Qu'Appelle Valley. His buckskin costume was collected by Alanson Skinner for the American Museum of Natural History, New York.

Smith, Naomi Southeastern Ojibwa, from the "Chippewas of Nawash" Cape Crocker bands of the Saugeen Peninsula, Ontario. A First Nations artisan and educator about the people of the Woodlands and Northeastern area from an historical and contemporary perspective, she is accomplished in beadwork, quillwork, moosehair embroidery, and basket-making. She has featured in Canadian exhibitions, at the 2010 Vancouver Winter Olympics, and showcases her work at the Smithsonian Institution, Washington, D.C. once a year.

Chief Topinabee or He Who Sits Quietly (1758–1826) Noted Potawatomi chief born in his father's village on the St. Joseph River, MI, in 1758. He signed the Treaty of Greenville in 1795. His son, also called Topinabee, met Lewis Cass and Pierre Manard in 1832 on the St. Joseph. He was succeeded by Leopold Pokagon.

Above Left: Shingabawassin as copied for McKenney and Hall.

Above Right: Naomi Smith. She is wearing a cloth "strap dress" reported to have been made at White Earth, MN, in the early 20th century. The dress has two straps hanging from the shoulders. It is decorated with beadwork in otter-tail designs. She also wears a fine contemporary trade silver brooch.

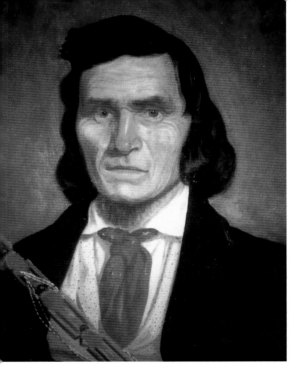  

Above, L–R: Chief Topinabee (He Who Sits Quietly). Painting by Van Sanden, a 19th century Dutch itinerant painter.

Wabanquot, c. 1890.

Wah-bo-jeeg (White Fisher) II or III, Gull Lake Band.

Valliere, Wayne or Minogiizhig A Lac du Flambeau Ojibwa, he is one of only three birchbark canoe makers in Wisconsin by 2015. Valliere is an artist and language and culture educator at the Lac du Flambeau Public School. He views canoe projects as a way to pass on Ojibwa heritage to youngsters.

Wabanquot (c. 1830–1898) Ojibwa chief, born Gull Lake, MN, he succeeded his father as chief of the band. After 1862 the Gull Lake Band was moved to the Leech Lake Reservation and later to the White Earth Reservation. He became a convert to the Episcopalian Church and later to the Catholic Church.

Wabbicommicot (d. 1768) Mississauga Ojibwa. He was one of 12 Ojibwa chiefs who met Sir William Johnson at Niagara in August 1764 at a council attended by over 2,000 Indians. His presence was at the behest of Major Gladwin in recognition of his dispersal of hostile Indians at the siege of Detroit during the Pontiac War. Johnson asked Wabbicommicot to resettle in his old haunts near Toronto providing his followers with preferential treatment and trade goods by way of hoping to pacify Pontiac and splitting his confederacy through these intermediaries. Unlike Amherst, Bouquet, and Gladwin who had advocated a policy of eliminating Indians through introducing disease and use of liquor, Johnson by contrast had a degree of respect for Indians through his relationship with the Mohawks and particularly the Brants.

Wah-bo-jeeg or White Fisher II (c. 1747–1793) Ojibwa chief and warrior, he was born near the western end of Lake Superior. His father had fought with the French at Quebec in 1759. His family had intermarried with

the Dakota during times of peace and he was related to Wapasha, a famous Sioux chief. His daughter and son became prominent in the Sault Ste. Marie area. She married a Scots-Irish fur trader, John Johnston, and her eldest daughter married Henry Rowe Schoolcraft. Her knowledge of the Ojibwa language and legends, which she shared with Schoolcraft, formed part of the source material for Longfellow's *The Song of Hiawatha*. Schoolcraft was part of the Lewis Cass expedition to establish the source of the Mississippi in 1820 and appointed U.S. Indian Agent in upper Michigan in 1822.

Warren, William W. (1825–1853) Born La Pointe, WI, of mixed blood Ojibwa, he was bilingual and educated in American schools. Moving to Minnesota in 1845, he collected oral traditions of the Ojibwa people and his important work *History of the Ojibway People, Based upon Traditional and Oral Statements* (1885) was published posthumously by the Minnesota Historical Society. He married Mathilda Aitken, also of mixed descent, who died in 1902.

Yellow Quill or O-zah-wah-sko-gwan-na-be (d. 1910). He was the Manitoba Saulteaux leader of the Portage Band who broke off from Treaty No. 1 negotiations at Lower Fort Garry in 1871. In 1876 at Round Plain, Manitoba, he renegotiated with Lt. Gov. Alexander Morris. Yellow Quill's descendants and his band are today mostly at Swan Lake Reserve, Manitoba. Another Yellow Quill signed Treaty No. 4 in 1874 with Morris at Qu'Appelle in Saskatchewan, and he has descendants at Kinistino and Nut Lake, recently renamed Yellow Quill Reserve. However, some believe he may have been the same man as at Treaty No. 1 and had started an Ojibwa exodus into Saskatchewan, then later returned to Swan Lake where he died in 1910.

Chapter 6: Gazetteer

Below: The granite slab on which the Agawa Bay pictographs were inscribed. Weather and water have eroded them, but they are still visible.

Agawa Bay Some 55 miles northwest of Sault Ste. Marie, Ontario, Agawa Bay lies on the north shore of Lake Superior. It is the site of famous pictographs publicized by Selwyn Dewdney in 1959, although they had been reported by ethnologist Henry Schoolcraft in the 19th century. Difficult to date with precision, the red ochre paintings include an image of a mythical creature, Mishepishu, a canoe with figures and early images of horses. The pictographs were made in the 17th and 18th centuries. Known to the French "coureurs du bois" by the 1660s, the local Ojibwa advised explorers Radisson and Groseilliers to follow the Lake Superior shoreline north to Michipicoten, and then by way of the Missinaibi and Moose rivers to James Bay. Both the Hudson's Bay and, later, North West companies made use of this route.

Cheboygan Today's "Gateway to the Waterways" was originally an Ojibwa settlement on Lake Huron at the mouth of the Cheboygan River. Southeast of Macinaw City in Michigan, Cheboygan saw its first European settler in 1844. It became a city in 1889.

Fort Crawford At Prairie du Chien, WI, at the junction of the Wisconsin River and the Mississippi. It is the site of an early French fur trade post and Fort Shelby in the War of 1812. Renamed Fort McKay after its capture by the British, it was rebuilt as Fort Crawford subsequently. Three treaties between the U.S. and native tribes were signed here.

Fort William Constructed in 1803 by the North West Company after its earlier headquarters at Grand Portage came under U.S. jurisdiction, the fort was located at the mouth of the Kaministiquia River. Today, the Fort William Historical Park, Ontario, contains a reconstruction of a trade post of the early 19th century.

Grand Portage At the beginning of the 18th century Grand Portage became a major center of the French fur trade, an outlet to Lake Superior from a waterway corridor that led to Lake of the Woods. Later, it was in British hands 1760–1796; now it's an Indian Reservation for the local Ojibwa Grand Portage Band (see photos overleaf).

La Pointe Originally a French trading post founded in 1693, La Pointe is on Madelaine Island in Chequamegon Bay on the Lake Superior shore of northern Wisconsin, an important area in Ojibwa history and culture. It was a refuge area for natives fleeing from the Iroquios in the 17th century and later Ojibwa arrived searching for new hunting and trading areas.

Top: The importance of the rivers and waterways in a wilderness without roads cannot be overstated. This 1857 watercolor by William Henry Edward Napier is titled *Poling up, Kaministikwia River above Fort William*. Today we use a different spelling — Kaministiquia — for the river that reaches Lake Superior at Thunder Bay.

Above: An untitled 1857 watercolor, this shows Fort William from the south side of Kaminitiquia River by John Arnot Fleming.

Opposite, Below: Pictographs at Agawa Bay: mythical creature Mishepishu and canoe figures.

Above: Grand Portage National Monument in northern Minnesota preserves another important fur trade location on Lake Superior. A difficult stretch of the River Pigeon was bypassed by a haulage route between Grand Portage and Fort Charlotte. In 1857 Seth Johnson painted an Ojibwa wigwam here.

Below: From the records of the Lac du Flambeau Agency — part of the Office of Indian Affairs — this sheet shows the sort of housing available to the Ojibwa of the 1920s.

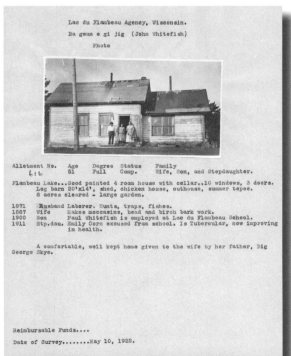

La Pointe became a center for settlement and native culture from where they spread inland during the early 18th century. During the 1850s the Ojibwa in the area divided into two groups, one Catholic under Chief Buffalo who established Red Cliff Reservation, and the traditionalists who moved to the Bad River Reservation at Odanah. The area today remains a spiritual center for the Ojibwa with a revival of interest in the Midewiwin.

Lac Court Oreilles (Lake Short Ears) Possibly known to Europeans as early as the 1660s, it was a permanent Ojibwa village site after their inland migration from Chequamegon Bay during the first half of the 18th century, and was visited by Jonathan Carver in 1767 and Schoolcraft in 1831. The lake's name derives from French trappers who thought the local Ottawa clipped their ears. Today's reservation was established by treaty in 1854 and it remains an important and predominantly native area of Wisconsin.

Lac du Flambeau (Torch Lake) The Ojibwa established a permanent settlement at Lac du Flambeau in 1745 after defeating the Dakota at Mole Lake in present northern Wisconsin. It became a hub in a trading and hunting network in the area's watershed. The North West Company had a fur trade post there by 1792. The reservation was established by treaty in 1854, and although land was lost in the 1880s, the tribe has recently purchased Strawberry Island in the lake, the site of a victory over the Dakota.

Lachine (alternatively, La Chine or "China") Located on the southwestern part of Montreal Island, it was the launch point for fur traders, particularly after the general peace treaty of 1701. Named by René-Robert Cavelier de La Salle, who believed he would find a passage to China, today it is a borough of Montreal City.

Lake of the Woods At the junction of the Precambrian Shield western Parklands, where the provinces of Manitoba and Ontario join

with Minnesota, lies Lake of the Woods with more than 14,000 islands and a shoreline greater than that of Lake Superior. During the 1730s it was the headquarters of La Vérendrye's expeditions west and the end of a waterway corridor from Lake Superior used by the North West and Hudson's Bay companies. It was once home for Cree and Assiniboine and, later, Ojibwa.

Lower Fort Garry Following the destruction by floods in 1826 of the original Fort Garry at the forks of the Red and Assiniboine rivers, the Hudson's Bay Company rebuilt the fort some 20 miles farther north on the west bank of the Red River — Lower Fort Garry.

Top: The Lac du Flambeau Museum and Cultural Center is named after tribal member George W. Brown, Jr.

Above: Lower Fort Garry Historic Site, Manitoba. It became a National Historic Site in 1950.

Inset: The blockhouse at Fort Crawford and footings for other buildings (see entry on p. 141).

Above: *Numbering the Indians*, Wikwemikong, Manitoulin Island, Ontario, August 16, 1856, after William Armstrong.

Below: Fort Mackinac marker.

Opposite, from Top: A reconstruction of Fort Michilimackinac in Mackinaw City, Michigan.

Another view of Lower Fort Garry Historic Site.

Mille Lacs trading post.

The Red River settlement had become an important center for redundant Métis fur trade employees created by the merger of the Hudson's Bay and the North West companies in 1821. Due to the declining fur trade, and following violence between the partisans of each company, Henry Bathurst, the British Secretary of State for War and the Colonies, ordered the companies to stop fighting and, in July 1821, to merge. Lower Fort Garry never proved as popular a site as the earlier fort and few initially moved from the original site. A Métis government continued until the founding of the Province of Manitoba in 1870. On August 3, 1871, the first treaty in Western Canada was set up between the federal government and chiefs of the Ojibway (Saulteaux) and Swampy Cree First Nations at Lower Fort Garry.

Mackinac An island at the eastern end of of the Straits of Mackinac in Lake Huron between the upper and lower Michigan peninsulas. Strategically positioned for the fur trade with a mixed population of Europeans, Indians, and Métis during the 18th century. British forces left the island in 1794, but captured it again during the War of 1812.

HISTORIC FORT MACKINAC

Mackinac Island has been called the most historic spot in the Middle West. Fort Mackinac was first built by the British in 1780–81. It was not until 1796, thirteen years after the end of the Revolutionary War, that the British relinquished this fort to the Americans. At the outbreak of the War of 1812 the British seized the island and built Fort George. This fort, which you see to the north beyond the Rifle Range, was renamed Fort Holmes by the Americans who reoccupied the island in 1815. Troops garrisoned Fort Mackinac until 1895.

Michilimackinac First, a French fort (built around 1715) and later British (after 1761) located on the northern tip of the lower peninsula of Michigan adjacent to the Straits of Mackinac. Ojibwa captured the fort in 1763 killing most of the British inhabitants. During the American Revolution the British moved the fort to the adjacent Mackinac Island.

Manitoulin Island (Spirit Island) Set adjacent to the northern shore of Lake Huron in Ontario, Manitoulin Island is the largest freshwater island in the world and home for Ottawa (Odawa), Ojibwa, and Potawatomi bands. Known to French Jesuits from 1648, and visited by refugees fleeing from Iroquois war parties during the 17th century. The population was reduced by smallpox. Island warriors of the "Three Fires" aided the British during the War of 1812. Between 1836 and 1862 the island was ceded to the Crown (Government of Canada), but two bands (now joined as one Wikwemikong) refused to sign, so the eastern part of the island remains unceded. The six reserve bands on the island have become famous for the porcupine-quilled birchbark crafts produced for curio hunters for many years.

Mille Lacs Originally the homeland of several branches of the Dakota (Sioux) at the head of the Rum River in present-day central

Minnesota, the Ojibwa had removed the Dakota from the vicinity by the mid-18th century. The reservation was established by 1855 but today the Mille Lacs Band is fragmented into about 10 communities around the southern end of the lake and at Big Sandy Lake, East Lake, and a number centering in Pine County.

Nipigon An area known to the Cree and Ojibwa ancestors for the production of copper tools. French arrived in the late 1650s and traveled from Lake Superior along the Nipigon River to Lake Nipigon, one of the largest lakes in Ontario. Both the Hudson's Bay and North West companies maintained posts on Lake Nipigon.

Ottawa River Crucial link with the Mattawa River, Lake Nipissing, French River to Lake Huron, a quicker and shorter canoe route to the Western Great Lakes than the route via the St. Lawrence and Lakes Ontario and Erie.

Sault Ste. Marie Ancestors of the Ojibwa settled near the rapids more than 2,000 years ago attracted by the abundant whitefish filled waters. The French called the area the "Sault" meaning "leap" or "fall" and had established a Jesuit mission there by the 1650s. Located at the junction of Lakes Huron and Superior it was strategically positioned during the colonial conflicts and for competing fur trade companies.

Upper Fort Garry Four forts built at the junction of the Red and Assiniboine rivers where the present-day city

Left, from Top: Moose Mountain, Nipigon Bay after George Harlow White.

John Elliott Woolford's watercolor of the Mattawa River.

Sault Ste. Marie (from the South Side) after George Harlow White.

of Winnipeg (incorporated in 1874) now stands. The first was established by Le Vérendrye in 1738 as a base for further western exploration. The second, called Fort Gibraltar, was built by the North West Company in 1806 but seized by the employees of the Hudson's Bay Company from nearby Fort Douglas built in opposition in 1813. In June 1816 the "Nor'Westers" and their allies captured Fort Douglas killing the Hudson's Bay Company governor and 20 men at Seven Oaks a few miles from the fort. Lord Selkirk then restored order with the aid of Swiss mercenary soldiers. In 1821 the two trading companies merged and the fort was taken over by the Hudson's Bay Company and renamed Fort Garry, but it was destroyed by floods in 1826 and rebuilt in 1836. The fort remained the seat of government for the District of Assiniboia and the Red River settlement until 1870.

Its name lives on as The Fort Garry Horse, a Canadian Army Reserve armored regiment that fought with distinction in two world wars.

Below: Near Ste. Marie, after William Armstrong, 1913.

Bottom: Upper Fort Garry. Winnipeg, Manitoba.

Canadian Bands, Populations, and Maps

POPULATIONS OF FIRST NATION TREATY BANDS FOR MISSISSAUGA, NORTHERN OJIBWA, AND SAULTEAUX INCLUDING PLAINS OJIBWA, FOR ONTARIO AND MANITOBA, CANADA

Key to predominent cultural, linguistic groups:
Cree
M = Mississiauga or Southeastern Ojibwa
NO = Northern Ojibwa
S = Saulteaux
PO = Plains Ojibwa
Potawatomi = Potawatomi
M* = Mississauga plus Ottawa and Potawatomi
Da = Dakota or Eastern Sioux
I = Iroquois
D = Delaware
A = Algonkin

Band	Population		Prominent
	2005	1970	Cultural Group
ONTARIO			
Albany	3,843	1,346	Cree
Alderville (Alnwick)	976	211	M
Attawapiskat	2,810	1,040	Cree
Batchewana	2,209	401	NO
Beausoleil (Christian Island)	1,702	570	M
Big Grassy	619	212	S
Big Island	—	163	S
Brunswick House	624	198	NO + Cree
Caldwell	248	74	Potawatomi
Cape Crocker	2,138	758	M
Caribou Lake	897	404	NO + Cree

Band	Population 2005	1970	Prominent Cultural Group
Chapleau Cree	382	37	Cree
Chapleau Ojibway	—	13	NO
Chippewas of Georgina Island	672	195	M
Chippewas of Kettle & Stony Point	2,011	721	M
Chippewas of Rama	1,500	489	M
Chippewas of Sarnia	1,956	641	M
Chippewas of the Thames	2,266	939	M
Cockburn Island	—	33	M*
Constance Lake	1,429	438	Cree
Couchiching	1,925	585	S
Curve Lake (Mud Lake)	1,744	632	M
Dalles	—	89	S
Deer Lake	1,043	1,430	NO + Cree
Dokis	963	209	M
Eagle Lake	495	146	S
Flying Post	158	42	NO + Cree
Fort Hope	2,115	1,426	NO
Fort Severn	596	236	Cree
Fort William	1,723	410	NO
Garden River	2,121	604	M
Gibson	671	206	I
Golden Lake	1,909	475	A
Grassy Narrows	1,235	485	S
Gull Bay	1,029	368	NO
Henvey Inlet	554	165	M
Hiawatha (Rice Lake)	483	121	M
Iroquois of St. Regis	10,217	2,963	I
Iskatewizaagegan see Shoal Lake No. 39			
Islington now Wabaseemoong	1,665	622	S
Lac des Mille Lacs	506	71	NO
Lac La Croix	388	161	S
Lac Seul	2,679	1,153	NO
Long Lake No. 58	1,199	584	NO
Long Lake No. 77	770	289	NO
Magnetawan	218	52	NO
Magnettawan	—	3	
Martin Falls	577	237	NO
Matachewan	504	130	NO + Cree
Mattagami	443	139	NO
Michipicoten	728	154	NO
Missanabie Cree	358	62	Cree
Mississauga	1,005	284	M
Mississaugas of the Credit	1,681	546	M
Mitaajigamiing see Strangecoming			
Mohawks of the Bay of Quinte	7,533	2,111	I
Moose Deer Point	443	128	M
Moose Factory	3,570	1,055	Cree

Band	Population 2005	1970	Prominent Cultural Group
Moravian of the Thames	1,077	423	D
Munceys of the Thames	523	187	D
Naicatchewenin	346	145	S
Nautkamegwanning see Whitefish Bay			
New Post	—	48	Cree
Nicickousemenecaning	256	72	S
Nipigon	—	58	NO
Nipissing	2,078	511	M
Northwest Angle No. 33	438	158	S
Northwest Angle No. 37	339	85	S
Oneidas of the Thames	5,127	2,011	I
Osnaburgh	1,486	901	NO
Parry Island	384	347	M
Pays Plat	202	23	NO
Pic Heron Bay	944	336	NO
Pic Mobert	794	301	NO
Pikangikum	2,053	764	NO
Rainy River	816	365	S
Rat Portage	316	310	S
Red Rock	1,417	254	NO
Rocky Bay	291	202	NO
Sabaskong	668	229	S
Sandpoint	161	29	NO
Saugeen	1,559	737	M
Scugog	185	59	M
Seine River	668	331	NO
Serpent River	1,141	337	M
Shawanaga	519	118	M
Sheguiandah	313	91	M*
Sheshegwaning	370	148	M
Shoal Lake No. 39 now Iskatewizaagegan	546	187	S
Shoal Lake No. 40	516	220	S
Six Nations of the Grand River Band	23,902	8,680	I
Spanish River No. 1)		776	M
Spanish River No. 2) 2,290		86	M
Spanish River No. 3)		12	M
Spanish River No. 4)		17	M
Strangecoming now Mitaajigamiing	142	23	S
Sucker Creek	701	180	M*
Thessalon	566	89	M
Timagami	650	160	NO + Cree
Trout Lake	1,278	1,945	NO + Cree
Wabaseemoong see Islington			
Wabauskang	251	67	S
Wabigoon	519	129	S
Wahnapitae	356	17	NO

Band	Population		Prominent
	2005	1970	Cultural Group
Walpole Island	3,952	1,577	M*
Weenusk	512	211	Cree
West Bay	2,192	812	M*
Whitefish Bay now Nautkamegwanning	1,109	363	M
Whitefish Lake	866	209	M*
Whitefish River	1,068	312	M*
Whitesand	1,059	265	NO
Wikwemikong	6,880	2,786	M*
Including Southbay			M*
MANITOBA			
Barren Lands	919	505	Cree
Berens River	2,531	719	S
Birdtail Sioux	686	187	Da
Bloodvein	1,364	339	S
Brokenhead	1,547	434	S
Buffalo Point	110	25	S
Chemahawin	1,506	337	Cree
Churchill	926	346	Cree
Crane River	812	154	S
Cross Lake	6,470	1,634	Cree
Dakota Plains	237	—	Da
Dakota Tipi	280	—	Da
Ebb and Flow	2,233	468	S
Fairford now Pauingassi	2,539	720	S
Fisher River	3,023	1,065	S
Fort Alexander now Sagkeeny	6,486	1,634	Cree
Fox Lake	998	197	Cree
Gamblers	149	28	PO
Garden Hill, Island Lake	3,748	1,265	Cree
God's Lake	2,242	1,041	Cree
Grand Rapids	1,394	273	S
Hollow Water	1,479	358	S
Jackhead	277	256	S + Cree
Keeseekowenin	992	302	PO
Lake Manitoba	1,659	479	S
Lake St. Martin	2,088	581	S
Little Black River	906	194	S
Little Grand Rapids	1,322	733	S
Little Saskatchewan	1,009	323	S
Long Plain	3,362	775	PO
Long Plain Sioux	572	224	Da
Mathias Colomb	3,119	908	Cree
Moose Lake	1,635	264	Cree
Nelson House	4,882	1,448	Cree
Norway House	6,229	1,934	Cree
Oak Lake	295	272	Da

Band	Population		Prominent
	2005	1970	Cultural Group
Oak River Sioux, Sioux Valley	1,079	899	Da
Oxford House	2,427	810	Cree
Pauingassi see Fairford			
Peguis	7,846	2,060	S + PO
Pine Creek	2,539	549	S
Poplar River	1,320	392	S + Cree
Red Sucker Lake	879	235	Cree
Rolling River	893	309	PO
Roseau River	2,069	725	PO
Sagkeeny see Fort Alexander			
St. Theresa Point	3,168	913	Cree
Sandy Bay	5,164	1,348	PO
Shammatawa	1,238	430	Cree
Shoal River	603	502	S
Split Lake	2,946	866	Cree
Swan Lake	1,166	454	PO
The Pas	4,815	999	Cree
Valley River	427	369	S
Wasagamack	1,570	381	Cree
Waterhen now Skownan	677	295	S
Waywayseecappo	2,204	706	PO
York Factory	1,048	331	Cree

NB: For Saskatchewan see Plains Ojibwa

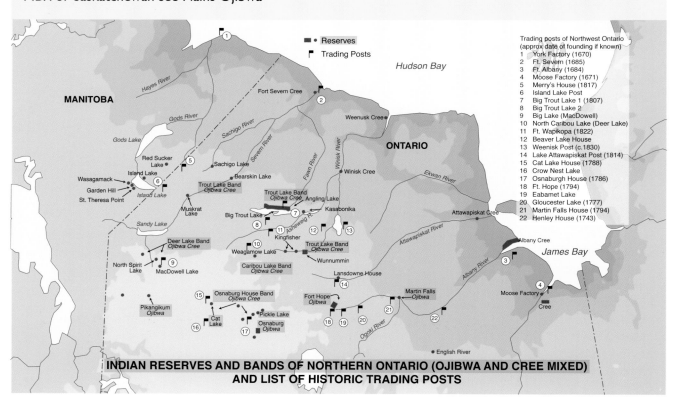

INDIAN RESERVES AND BANDS OF NORTHERN ONTARIO (OJIBWA AND CREE MIXED) AND LIST OF HISTORIC TRADING POSTS

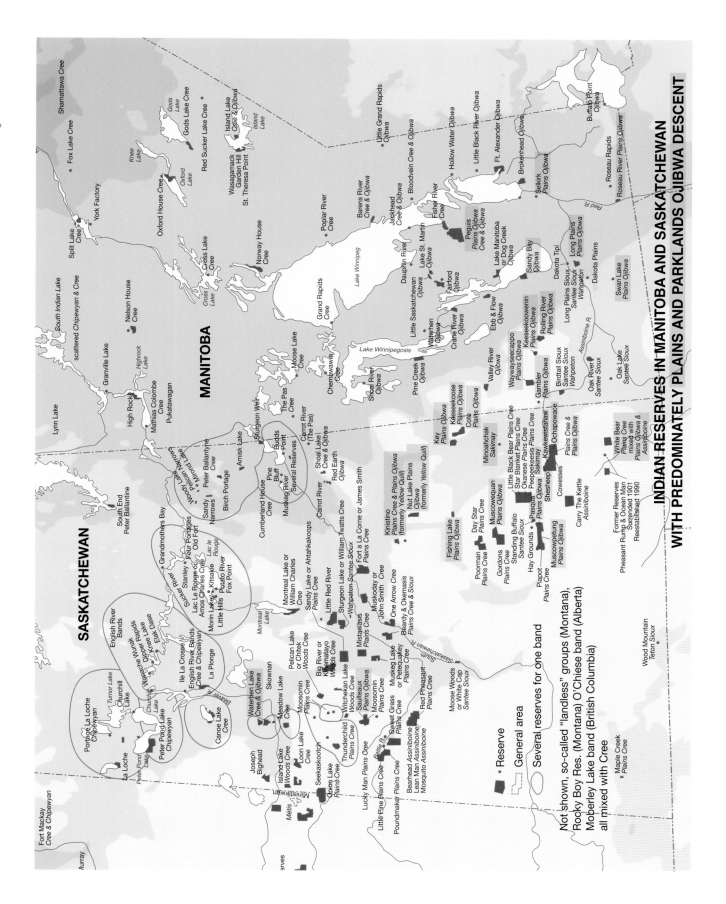

INDIAN RESERVES IN MANITOBA AND SASKATCHEWAN WITH PREDOMINATELY PLAINS AND PARKLANDS OJIBWA DESCENT

• Reserve

General area

Several reserves for one band

Not shown, so-called "landless" groups (Montana),
Rocky Boy Res. (Montana) O'Chiese band (Alberta)
Moberley Lake band (British Columbia)
all mixed with Cree

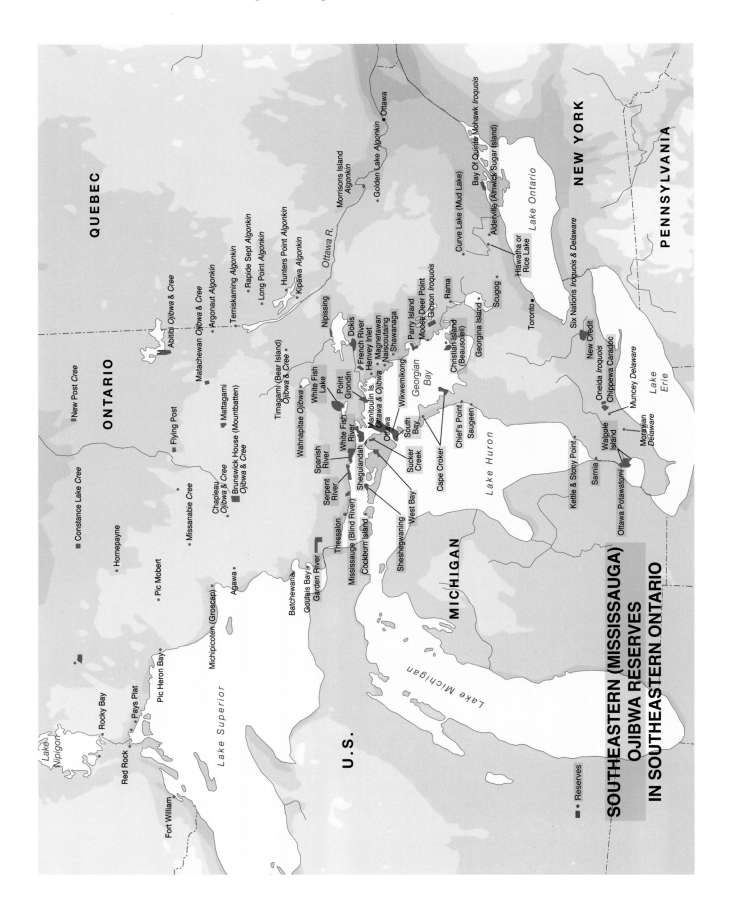

SOUTHEASTERN (MISSISSAUGA)
OJIBWA RESERVES
IN SOUTHEASTERN ONTARIO

■ Reserves

QUEBEC

ONTARIO

NEW YORK

PENNSYLVANIA

MICHIGAN

U.S.

Lake Nipigon

Lake Superior

Lake Michigan

Lake Huron

Georgian Bay

Lake Ontario

Lake Erie

Ottawa R.

Fort William
Red Rock
Rocky Bay
Pays Plat
Pic Heron Bay
Michipicoten (Groscap)
Pic Mobert
Hornepayne
Agawa
Batchewana
Goulais Bay
Garden River
Constance Lake Cree
Missanabie Cree
New Post Cree
Flying Post
Chapleau Ojibwa & Cree
Brunswick House (Mountbatten) Ojibwa & Cree
Mattagami
Matachewan Ojibwa & Cree
Abititi Ojibwa & Cree
Argonaut Algonkin
Temiskaming Algonkin
Rapide Sept Algonkin
Long Point Algonkin
Hunters Point Algonkin
Kipawa Algonkin
Morrisons Island Algonkin
Golden Lake Algonkin
Ottawa

Timagami (Bear Island) Ojibwa & Cree
Wahnapitae Ojibwa
White Fish Lake
Point Grondin
White Fish River
Spanish River
Serpent River
Thessalon
Cockburn Island
Mississauge (Blind River)
Sheguiandah
West Bay
Sheshegwaning
Manitoulin Is.
Ottawa & Ojibwa
Ottawa
Nipissing
Dokis
French River
Henvey Inlet
Magnetawan
Naiscoutaing
Shawanaga
Parry Island
South Bay
Wikwemikong
Sucker Creek
Cape Croker
Chief's Point
Saugeen
Moose Deer Point
Gibson Iroquois
Christian Island (Beausoleil)
Georgina Island
Rama
Scugog
Curve Lake (Mud Lake)
Hiawatha or Rice Lake
Toronto
Alderville
Bay Of Quinte Mohawk Iroquois
Alnwick (Sugar Island)
New Credit
Six Nations Iroquois & Delaware
Oneida Iroquois
Chippewa Caradoc
Muncey Delaware
Moravian Delaware
Walpole Island
Sarnia
Kettle & Stony Point
Ottawa Potawatomi

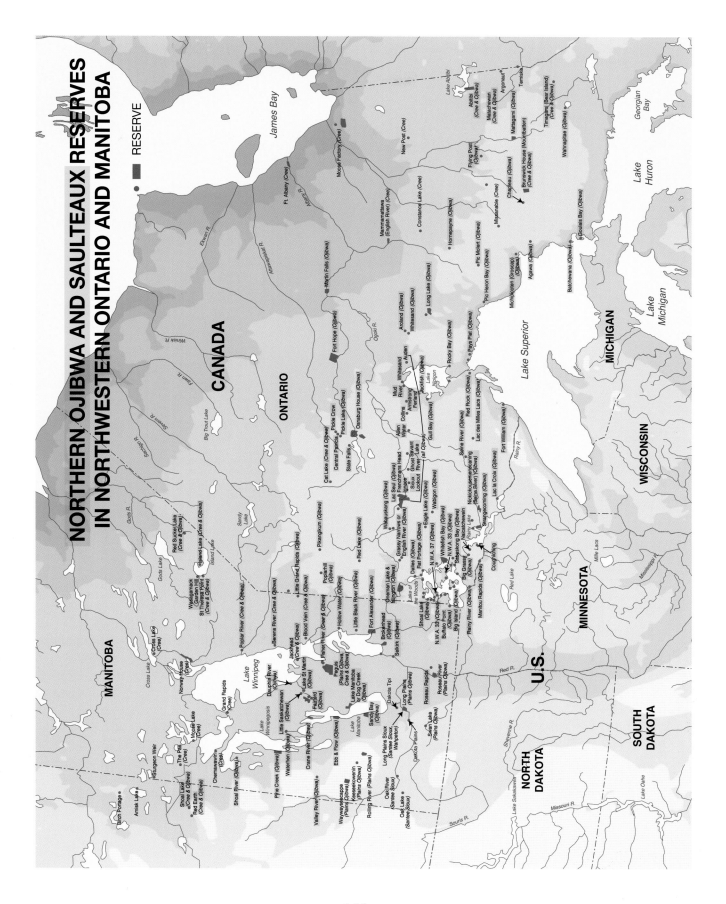

Bibliography

Adney, E.T., and Chapelle, H.I.: "The Bark Canoes and Skin Boats of North America," *U.S. National Museums Bulletin* 230; Smithsonian Institution Press, Washington D.C., 1964.

Armstrong, Benj., and Wentworth, Thos. P.: *Early Life Among the Indians;* Bowron Press, Asland, WI, 1892.

Barrett, S.A.: *The Dream Dance of the Chippewa and Menomini of Northern Wisconsin, Vol. 1;* Milwaukee Public Museum, WI, 1911.

Brownstone, Arni: "Spirit of the Plains"; *Rotunda Magazine* 37:3 pp14–21, Royal Ontario Museum, Toronto, ON, 2005.

Chandler, Milford G. et al: *Art of the Great Lakes Indians;* Flint Institute of the Arts, Flint, MI, 1973.

Clifton, James A.: *The Prairie People;* University of Iowa Press, 1998.

Danziger, Edmund Jefferson, Jr.: *The Chippewas of Lake Superior;* University of Oklahoma Press, Norman, OK, 1979.

Densmore, Francis: "Chippewa Customs"; *Bulletin 86;* Bureau of American Ethnography, Washington, D.C., 1929.

Densmore, Francis: "Chippewa Music"; *Bulletin 45;* Bureau of American Ethnography, Washington, D.C., 1910.

Dewdney, Selwyn: *The Sacred Scrolls of the Southern Ojibwa;* Glenbow-Alberta Institute, Calgary, University of Toronto Press, Toronto, ON, 1975.

Driver, Harold E.: *Indians of North America,* pp.18, 57, 58, map 2; University of Chicago Press, 2nd edition, 1972.

Dunning, R.W.: *Social and Economic Change and the Northern Ojibwa;* University of Toronto Press, Toronto, ON, 1959.

Guy, Camil: *L'Organisation socio-territoriale des Indiens de Weymontaching;* unpublished ms deposited in National Museum of Man, Ottawa, ON, 1966.

Hickerson, Harold: *The Chippewa and their Neighbors: A Study in Ethnohistory;* Holt, Rinehart and Winston, Inc., New York, 1970.

Hodge, F.W. (ed): *Handbook of the Indians of Canada;* appx to 10th Report of the Geographic Board of Canada; King's Printer, Ottawa, ON, 1913. (Can. Sess. Pap. 12th Parl. 1st Sess., vol. 15, 1911–12)

Hoffman, W.J.: "The Midewiwin or Grand Medicine Society of the Ojibwa"; *7th Annual Report,* Bureau of American Ethnography, Washington, D.C., 1891.

Opposite: Sha-có-pay, The Six, Chief of the Plains Ojibwa, painted by George Catlin at Fort Union (in present-day Montana), in 1832. The fringed hair style was typically Plains Ojibwa. Roundels of quillwork or beadwork were popular on men's shirts of the Plains Ojibwa and other northeastern Plains peoples, with perhaps Subarctic connections.

Above: Charles Albert "Chief" Bender (1884–1954) was born in Crow Wing County, MN, to a German father and Ojibwa mother. A pitcher of great renown — and a three times World Series champion (1910, 1911, 1913) — he played for the Philadelphia Athletics (1903–1914), Baltimore Terrapins (1915), and Philadelphia Phillies (1916–1917) before a season coaching for the Chicago White Sox (1925). He was elected to the Baseball Hall of Fame in 1953.

Howard, James: *The Plains Ojibwa or Bungi*; University of South Dakota, Vermilion, SD, 1965.

Johnson, Michael, and Hook, Richard: *Encyclopedia of Natives Tribes of North America*, 2nd Edition; Firefly Books Inc., Buffalo, NY, 2014.

Josephy, Alvin M.: *The Boy Artist of the Red River*; American Heritage Publishing Co. Inc., New York, 1970.

King, J.C.H.: *Thunderbird and Lightning, Indian Life in Northeastern North America 1600–1900*, The Trustees of the British Museum, London, 1982.

Kinietz, W. Vernon: "Chippewa Village: The Story of Katikitegun," *Bulletin 25*, Cranbrook Institute of Science, Bloomfield Hills, MI, 1947.

Kurz, Rudolph Friederich: *Journal of Rudolph Friederich Kurz, An account of his experiences among the fur traders and American Indians on the Mississippi and Upper Missouri River during the years 1846 to 1852*; ed J.H.B. Hewitt; Bison Books, University of Nebraska Press, Lincoln, NE, 1970.

Lyford, Carrie A.: *The Crafts of the Ojibwa (Chippewa)*; U.S. Office of Indian Affairs, Indian Handicrafts 5, Washington, D.C., 1943.

McKenney, Thomas L., and Hall, James: *History of the Tribes of North America* (three vols); John Grant, Edinburgh, 1933.

Peers, Laura: *The Ojibwa of Western Canada, 1780 to 1870*; University of Manitoba Press, Winnipeg, MB, 1994.

Penney, David: *Art of the American Indian Frontier*; University of Washington Press, Seattle, WA, 1992.

Pohrt, Richard, Jr. (ed): *Bags of Friendship: Bandolier Bags of the Great Lakes Indians*; Morning Star Gallery, Santa Fe, NM, 1996.

Quimby, George I.: *Indian Life in the Upper Great Lakes*; University of Chicago Press, 1960.

Ray, Arthur J.: *Indians of the Fur Trade*, pp28–32, fig.10; University of Toronto Press, Toronto, ON, 1974.

Ritzenthaler, R.E.: "The Building of a Chippewa Indian Birchbark Canoe"; *Bulletin of Public Museum of Milwaukee*, WI, 19(2), pp53–90, 1950.

Rogers, E.S.: *The Hunting Group—Hunting Territory Complex Among the Mistassini Indians*; National Museum of Canada Bulletin 195, Ottawa, ON, 1963.

Schmalz, Peter S.: *The Ojibwa of Southern Ontario*; University of Toronto Press, Toronto, ON, 1991.

Smith, Donald B.: *Mississauga Portraits, Ojibwa Voices from the 19th Century*; University of Toronto Press, Toronto, ON, 2013.

Smith, Donald B.: *Sacred Feathers, The Reverend Peter Jones (Kahkenaquonaby) and the Mississauga Indians*; University of Nebraska Press, Lincoln, NE, 1987.

Tanner, Helen Hornbeck (ed): *Atlas of Great Lakes Indian History*; University of Oklahoma Press, Norman, OK, 1986.

Vennum, Thomas, Jr.: *The Ojibwa Dance Drum, its History and Construction*; Smithsonian Institution Press, Washington, D.C., 1982.

Waugh, F.W.: "Canadian Aboriginal Canoes," *Canadian Field-Naturalist*, 33 pp22–33, Ottawa, ON, 1919.

White, Bruce: *We Are At Home*; Minnesota Historical Society Press, St. Paul, MN, 2007.

Index